Narcissistic Mothers

The truth about the problem with being the Daughter of a Narcissistic Mother and how to fix it. A guide for healing and recovering after narcissistic abuse

Dr. Theresa J. Covert

Copyright 2019 - All rights reserved.

This eBook was written to provide information on the subject matter "*Narcissistic Mothers: The Truth about the struggles of being the daughter of a narcissistic mother and a step by step guide to healing and recovering from narcissistic abuse* " that is as accurate and reliable as possible. Both the publisher and the author of this eBook are in no way experts on the topics discussed within, and any recommendations or suggestions that are made herein are for entertainment and informational purposes only. Professionals should be consulted as needed before undertaking any of the action endorsed herein. This declaration is deemed fair and valid by both the American Bar Association and the Committee of Publishers Association and is legally binding throughout the United States.

Furthermore, the transmission, duplication, or reproduction of any part of the following work, including specific information, will be considered an illegal act irrespective of if it is done electronically or in print. This extends to creating a secondary or tertiary copy of the work or a recorded copy without the written consent from the Publisher. All rights reserved.

The information in the following pages is generally considered to be a truthful and an accurate account of facts, and as such any inattention, use or misuse of the information on the part of the reader is the sole responsibility of the reader alone. There will be no scenarios in which the publisher or the original author of this work will be in any fashion deemed liable for any hardship or damages that may befall the reader after undertaking information described herein.

Additionally, the information in the following pages is intended only for informational purposes and should thus be thought of as universal. As befitting its nature, it is presented without an assurance regarding its prolonged validity or interim quality. Trademarks that are mentioned are done without written consent and can in no way be considered an endorsement from the trademark holder.

Table of Contents

Introduction 4

Chapter 1: Narcissistic Personality Disorder 8

Chapter 2: Types of Narcissism 19

Chapter 3: How to Recognize a Narcissistic Mother 32

Chapter 4: Behaviors of a Narcissistic Mother 39

Chapter 5: The Signs that you have a Narcissistic Mother 48

Chapter 6: Treatment for Children of Narcissistic Mothers 63

Chapter 7: Things Narcissistic Mothers Say for Mental Manipulation and Control 82

Chapter 8: Protection Tips 103

Chapter 9: Separating from a Narcissistic Mother 114

Chapter 10: How to HEAL from ABUSE! 118

Conclusion 130

Introduction

> **A NARCISSIST IS A CON ARTIST, THEY SELL YOU A DREAM AND DELIVER YOU A LIVING NIGHTMARE.**

Pride, arrogance, ego, and admiration; these are all feelings that are okay with some restraint. However, a narcissist is excessively proud and thinks that they are entitled to get anything that they want.

So, what is narcissism?

Narcissism has its origins in Greek mythology where there was a young man named Narcissus. He was a Greek hunter from Boeotia and the son of the river god and a nymph. He was a remarkably handsome person.

One day, Nemesis lured him to the edge of a lake where he fell in love with the water pool reflection of himself. Narcissus was so engrossed with admiring his reflection that he ended up drowning in the lake.

In this day and age, narcissism is a theory used in psychoanalysis; the psychoanalysis theory has its beginnings in the 1914 essay on narcissism by Sigmund Freud.

Also, the American Psychiatrist Association classifies narcissism as a mental disorder characterized by patterns of need for the admiration of others and a lack of empathy for others, a grandiose sense of self-importance and a sense of entitlement.

Narcissism is a personality trait disorder. Most psychologists and psychoanalysis experts agree that narcissism is a cultural and social problem that is on the increase in our world today.

However, most specialists in the field of psychology agree there is healthy narcissism; these specialists see healthy narcissism as a show of healthy self-love, and most experts also agree that the line between healthy self-love and narcissistic propensities is an extremely thin one and that healthy self-esteem can rapidly grow into narcissism without an individual's knowledge.

An obsession over one's physical appearance, traits, and achievements at unnatural levels can lead to a distraction from daily life and activities.

Narcissism Personality Disorder (NPD) is one of the three dark personalities together with Machiavellianism, and Psychopathy. These three dark personalities are referred to as the "dark triad." People with these three disorders exhibit malevolent qualities.

It will help at this point not confuse narcissism with egocentrism. Narcissists are all about their egos, just like the egocentrics, but there is a difference between a narcissist and an egocentric person. A narcissist only gets their fix of admiration or whatever supply it is that they need for the moment from someone else.

Dealing with narcissism is very difficult; this is because the people suffering from it do not see it as a problem. The people who suffer from narcissism believe that they are perfectly fine and healthy.

Any event or person that forces people living with Narcissistic Personality Disorder to double-check themselves will not produce change. They will still try to cover the facts about them as attacks and live on with their disorder.

Chapter 1: Narcissistic Personality Disorder

> **THE BEST TEST TO SEE IF SOMEONE IS A NARCISSIST, SAY NO TO THEM AND WATCH THEIR RESPONSE.**

Most experts in the field of psychiatry believe that Narcissistic Personality Disorder (NPD) cannot be cured. This means that people diagnosed with it will have the symptoms of the disorder all their lives and will have to continually work hard to deal with the behavioral difficulties caused by the disorder.

Although people diagnosed with NPD might experience relief of symptoms and might learn valuable coping strategies, they will still have some signs of the disorder for the rest of their lives. Also, most psychiatrists don't believe that medication works well to control any personality disorder, especially NPD.

Narcissism is a kind of belief a person has about themselves, that they are unique and more important than others around them. With this belief, they often act in particular ways and will do things to boost their image in the eyes of others.

The belief in their superiority over others is so deeply ingrained in narcissists that they experience many difficulties when dealing with other people as they will often treat everyone else as less important.

Narcissistic Personality Disorder (NPD), therefore, is the term that connotes a type of mental disorder wherein the individual affected has an exaggerated sense of self-importance.

Individuals affected with NPD have a deep need for reverence from others, though they lack empathy for others. Individuals affected with NPD do not present themselves for psychological treatment because they do not see that there is an issue with their conduct, even though they are aware that people around them constantly find them very difficult to deal with.

The criteria officially used for diagnosing Narcissistic Personality Disorder are described in the Diagnostic and Statistical Manual, Version Five (DSM-V). The DSM-V is the book mental health experts use to diagnose mental illnesses.

It is pertinent to note that some people might display signs of narcissistic tendencies but do not have full-blown NPD.

A few criteria for diagnosing NPD as described in the DSM-V are:

A. Antagonism, characterized by Grandiosity, and

B. Attention seeking.

The criteria described in the DSM-V can be explained through the actions of the particular individual suffering from NPD. An individual who is affected by NPD will only think of themselves. Their actions will reveal that they think only about themselves and seek to put down individuals around them.

For instance, an individual suffering from NPD may misrepresent their contribution to a work project while deprecating the commitment of a co-worker to the project. The individual might even steal the ideas of others and take credit for the ideas and actions of others. An individual suffering from NPD must be at the center of the universe at all times.

To be diagnosed with full-blown NPD means that a person must exhibit this attention-seeking behavior both over time and in many different circumstances. They must have exhibited it as a young adult, and they must have grown older without much change in their behavior. They exhibit attention-seeking with their family, at work, and in the community. This personality trait seems stable, no matter who they are with and what they are doing.

A person suffering from NPD cannot have their behaviors explained based upon how old they are. For example, many teenagers act like they are the center of the universe and may exaggerate their actions, but this can be explained as a normal stage in their psychological growth, which they will eventually outgrow. However, a person with NPD will never abandon their teenage behaviors. So for an adult, some acts are not considered normal. This is one of the reasons why personality disorders such as NPD are not diagnosed until a person is an adult.

Someone with NPD will seek attention and have a false sense of self no matter what their state of sobriety is. For instance, a person who behaves like a narcissist while drunk, but is a loving and healthy person while sober, would not be diagnosed with NPD because their behaviors are as a result of the alcohol in their system. Someone with NPD will act like a narcissist no matter what their state is.

Taken as a whole, when someone has NPD, they believe that they are the center of the universe and everything revolves around them and as such, they bear no regard for the feelings of people around them, along with the fact that they will not be empathetic with other people.

People suffering from NPD will do whatever they can to be the center of attention and show others how significant they are to the world. They will continue to show these traits throughout their whole lives. Usually, these traits start to show in their lives during adolescence, and they will carry these traits into adulthood.

It is estimated that up to 6.2% of the general population suffer narcissistic personality disorder and that men are more than twice as likely to be diagnosed as women.

How Narcissistic Personality Disorder Develops

As with any other mental illness or personality disorder, there are different explanations for NPD. The causes of NPD could show up independently or exist along with one another in someone's life; this will then encourage the development of NPD.

The first puzzle piece in the development of NPD is genetics. If a family member had NPD, it is quite likely that children and some other relatives might also develop the disorder. This is because of psychobiology; the idea that the brain and human behaviors are connected. If the brain is genetically wired in one way because of the genes a person has inherited from parents and grandparents, then a person is likely to inherit the genes that caused for the wiring to occur in such a way to create NPD. People who have a genetic predisposition are more likely to suffer from NPD than those without it.

The other trigger for NPD is parenting issues. If a person lives with a parent or in a family situation where they are overly pampered, treated continuously as unique, or given everything they ever ask for without any idea that there are limits, they are more likely to develop NPD. Children need boundaries and discipline, and without them, they will grow up with an unrealistic view of both themselves and how the world works. They incorporate the belief that they are special and perfect into their worldview.

On the other hand, people who grew up with parents who were especially harsh and never valued anything the child did can also develop NPD. The child develops a defense mechanism to offset the negative and constant criticism that they receive. Think of it like a pendulum swinging the other way. If the parent is overly harsh to the child, the child will start to overcompensate by believing that they are entitled to everything, that they are special, and that they deserve the world, just to combat the negativity that surrounds them every single day. This is generally thought to happen because the child may be overcompensating to try to prove their worth to their parent. They want to earn the parent's love and approval.

No matter which type of parent the person with NPD had, the parental behaviors began while the child was young, generally before the age of three.

A third factor that may be relevant to the development of NPD is society's ideas of who and what is important. For example, the idea that the most powerful, rich, and successful are more important than "ordinary people" has become an ingrained belief thanks to mass media's preoccupation with these types of people. In watching reality TV, people who are self-centered, selfish, and rude to others are idealized, whereas people who are caring and compassionate are often marginalized or completely ignored. Second, people receive more approval from outside influence when they are smarter, more prosperous, or have a higher status. This could cause people to work for this higher status so they can receive the same type of recognition. Last, there is a weakening of the community in our society. Children are not often brought up to believe they are part of something bigger than themselves, which leads to kids having more difficulty identifying with others. A grandiose self-image replaces their ability to empathize.

Usually, however, there is a mixture of both genetic factors and environmental factors, both personal and societal, at work with the development of any personality disorder. If a parent or other close family member has the personality disorder, the child will likely grow up both with a genetic link to get it and in an unstable home environment where the traits are more likely to develop. Because many of the traits have been shown to exist since childhood, it is easy to see why the disorder becomes so challenging to treat.

However, that doesn't mean there are not treatments or options for a person suffering from NPD or their families. The next chapter will give some clues into the current treatments available through modern medicine and psychiatry to handle Narcissistic Personality Disorder.

You will, undoubtedly, have heard of the term 'Ego'. It is naturally assumed that everyone has one; although some people's egos are much larger than others. Ego is an idea of your self-worth; in many people, this is a fragile item; easily affected by others and their opinions and views.

Your ego will be built upon your own beliefs and experiences throughout life; if you have always met with success, you are likely to have a bigger ego and be more confident. Likewise, those who often meet with failure will tend to have a diminished ego and be less confident in their abilities. Everything you undertake in life will help to build or diminish this ego; it is a moving, almost living thing, and this is an essential, healthy part of life.

Egoism is an extension of this principle; it believes that all actions and goals should relate to yourself; everything that you do should benefit you and help you to reach your own goals. Moving a stage past this and you become someone with NPD; when the achievement of your goals and the benefit of your actions focuses entirely on you. This should be regardless of the effect on those around you. Egoism is often disguised as kindness and generosity; giving someone else a gift without a reward can seem selfless; in fact, it is often a tool used by someone with NPD to manipulate and gain the support of others; the gift can later be mentioned to ensure a favor is provided when needed. A true egotist will not consider the thoughts of others; their interests lie only in what is good for them.

An ego which centers on your own needs above all others is essential for the creation of NPD. What is perhaps the most interesting thing about this is that it is agreed that someone is born without any ego. At the moment you are born, you do not have any preconceived ideas about the world, yourself, or even any knowledge. All these things are built upon from the moment you are born. Your first instincts will be to reach out and explore the world around you; in a baby, this is done through the senses; sight, touch, smell; hearing, and taste. At this point your ego is simply a reflection of what others think and do; if they praise you and smile at you then you will feel good about yourself, if they do not, you will feel bad about yourself. From this simple beginning, your ego will grow and will be fed by the images and experiences around you. From this standpoint, an egotist or someone likely to have a narcissistic personality is a product of society. Of course, this is a very simplistic approach as there are many other factors which will influence the development of NPD; the exact cause is not known but could be linked to your genes.

The definition of egoism is that the self-belief created by your ego is essential to ensuring you make the correct moral decisions and, therefore, behave by accepted moral standards.

Of course, these standards also extend to assist in understanding the development of NPD; egoism accepts that anyone should put themselves first and this self-belief should motivate all conscious actions; this means that self-interest is an acceptable conclusion to any action, which is exactly what someone with NPD does!

Selfishness is also a trait of someone with NPD; their desires are placed above all others. They see themselves as more important and worthy of success than anyone else, and this becomes a justification for being selfish. Almost everyone has been selfish at some point or the other in their life; it could be hanging onto a vital person because they need them rather than it being the best thing for the person or the relationship. Alternatively, it could be something more straightforward, like taking the last chocolate!

However, the traits of selfishness are sometimes essential in parts of life. Business leaders, in particular, need to put the interests of their company first to succeed. This can even be seen to be essential for preserving the jobs and welfare of their employees. However, putting the company's needs first will also ensure that their own needs are being given priority. The very traits which are essential for business success can start someone on the course to a narcissistic personality even if they do not develop NPD.

The economic acceptance of selfishness as an essential trait if the business shows the complications which arise when trying to establish the parameters and definition of someone suffering from NPD; in many walks of life their behavior will be akin with an extremely successful person. By this logic, selfishness is a desirable and even essential trait for those who wish to succeed.

To be genuinely selfish you need to be devoid of empathy or consideration for other people's feelings; this is, perhaps, the critical point at which someone will change from being considered socially 'normal' and having a personality disorder. Anyone who has NPD will be unable to establish empathy with those around them; this inevitably leads to the ability and desire to manipulate those around you as you lose the ability to respect their feelings or needs. This type of behavior is associated with those suffering from NPD as well as psychopaths.

It must be understood that, as with all personality traits, it is essential to have an awareness of self and to look out for your interests. Being selfish is necessary at times to ensure you stick to your principles, values, or simply to complete a job close to your heart. The crucial difference is understanding the effect this may have on others and choosing to do it anyway, despite the emotional and physical consequences. If you are never selfish, you will never stand up for anything you believe in and will be likely to spend your life following the herd, possibly never achieving your full potential.

It has been suggested that selfishness in adults can be created through a difficult childhood. Any child who has little or no praise or even acknowledgment of their existence is likely to retreat into their world. Some of these children will become recluses and socially inept for life; others will build their fantasy worlds to retreat into and escape the harshness of their life. These fantasy worlds will often revolve around having the control, power, and admiration that they are not receiving as a child. These worlds can be carried into adulthood, and a narcissistic personality will develop as the desire to be appreciated will eclipse all other feelings. Again, this development will be in conjunction with other influences and your genes.

Selfishness is a trait of someone with NPD; however, you can be selfish without having NPD. Aside from the healthy form of selfishness which has already been discussed; most people find themselves being selfish because of the demands and stresses of their own lives; it is not a fundamental desire to hurt others but rather a reaction to your environment. Selfish people tend to come across as selfish, while people with NPD are charming and will appear to fit in well, while being very accommodating. This is because they are manipulating and controlling people around them to obtain their own selfish needs. The difference in personality is both easy to spot and an essential part of the difference between someone who has NPD and someone who does not. After all, someone who truly has NPD will be very concerned with looking good to others; this will ensure they get the help they need to achieve their goals. They will appear trustworthy and unselfish when, in fact, they are the exact opposite; the problem is their charm and charisma will hide their true personality and motivation from you.

Chapter 2: Types of Narcissism

While we talk about narcissism in general terms, there is more than one type. In the real world, when you meet a narcissist face to face, there may be signs that match the way a narcissist behaves because most of the time, they are a mix of the various types. As with typical combinations, there is always the dominant type mixed with another.

To help you to determine which one is what, here's a brief rundown of each different type and their specific characteristics or personality traits:

Cerebral

A cerebral narcissist believes that they are better than anyone and that their intelligence far exceeds that of anyone else. They flaunt their intelligence and self-assumed superiority to be admired and envied by the rest. They know everything about, well, everything. They make it a point to have an opinion or suggestion for everything that you might throw at them. They will be happy to tell you stories that show off their sheer brilliance, whether the stories are real or just made up. They are pleased to point out everyone else's failings and will look down on and sneer at anyone who is of lower intelligence. Such people are so obsessed with their grey matter that they will go out of their way to take alarmingly good care of it, sometimes to the extent that it reflects badly on their health and physical prowess. Narcissism is very often associated with sexual stimulation. Cerebral narcissists rarely engage in sexual stimulation with others, as they prefer personal stimulation over the real deal. Therefore, it would not come as much of a surprise when I say that they prefer the anonymity and lack of intimacy that comes with pornography.

For this reason, they may choose porn over real close relationships. Besides maintaining a relationship with such people is a Herculean task in itself as they will always insist on being the intellectually superior one in the relationship and assume the right to control the other person's thoughts, emotions, and actions. Even then, these relationships will be extremely short-lived as they are continually looking for more superior people to associate with. Cerebral narcissists should not be confused with somatic narcissists.

Somatic

Somatic narcissists are more closely in touch with the Greek legend of Narcissus. They are all consumed by how beautiful they believe they are. You will often find somatic narcissists at a gym or somewhere else where they are working on their appearance. For them, it is all about their body and physique. They can be seen continuously flexing their muscles and bragging about their success in sporting events. They expect their body to be the source of their narcissistic supply and so they dress up immaculately and keep themselves well-groomed. Their narcissistic supply comes from how others react to how they look or from their sexual conquests – indeed, most somatic narcissists will have a long list of partners. They never cease to boast about their conquests in bed. Even though they may have bedded many partners, most of the sex is bound to be cold and emotionless. Eventually, the word partner begins to lose meaning, and they may be more aptly described as the victim. Cheating in marital life is something that you shouldn't put past a somatic narcissist. He is happiest when his narcissistic supply comes from multiple sources. They are quite dangerous as they know how to manipulate people both emotionally and through sexual intercourse. This tends to scar their spouse for life if they decide to be in a long-term relationship with them.

Overt

This form of narcissism manifests in grandiosity. They are preoccupied about having outstanding success in many areas, like brilliance, attractiveness, sense of power, ideal love, etc. Since they have an immense sense of grandiosity, they believe that they can only be fully appreciated by other people on their level of grandiosity. The overt narcissist always has to be in control of any situation. They are never wrong, and they will never be shy about making it clear that everything is about them and that everything has to be done the way they want it done. Their egos are super-sized, and they are not backward in showing it to you either. The overt narcissist can cut you up, physically or verbally and will not show a single second of remorse or guilt. Such people are interpersonally very exploitative and will not think twice before using someone to achieve their own needs. Although very arrogant on the inside, they are experts at masking their egotism within a false humility. They envy other people to a great extent and get jealous of their achievements, possessions, and relationships. They seriously lack empathy, and this makes them unfit to work in a group. They are usually loners.

They may be seen as being overconfident, and they are extrovert in their behavior – in fact, it would be easier to describe their personality as loud, noticeable, larger than life, and somewhat oppressive.

Covert

The covert narcissist exhibits all the normal traits you would expect to find in a narcissist but with one difference: they want someone to take care of them. They are best described as the shy form of narcissism. He has grand fantasies similar to other types of narcissists, but he lacks the drive to pull it off successfully. He is too timid to get what he wants and lacks self-confidence. He usually feels worthless at not being able to pull off exactly what he wanted. He faces large feelings of shame about the same thing. He rarely takes credit for his achievements. He openly admires successful people and secretly envies them. He is unlikely to accumulate appropriate friends and prefers to surround himself with inferior persons. Such people are hyper-vigilant to rejection and humiliation. They could be described as parasites, living off other people. They will typically exhibit some signs of an illness that needs taking care of, and that is why they can never be what you want. They don't want to take responsibility for anything and will look for a partner who is strong, successful, and intelligent, one that can run their lives while they don't need to contribute anything. Covert narcissists will sometimes pair up with the overt narcissist.

Unprincipled

The unprincipled narcissist does not have a conscience and cannot seem to tell the difference between what's right and what's wrong. They care very little about laws, values, and conventions and stay just within the boundaries of the law. They exploit others without the slightest bit of remorse because they consider other people as inferior to them anyway. This unprincipled lifestyle makes them more than willing to risk harm, and they are remarkably fearless in the face of danger. Their malicious and diabolic tendencies are easily visible, and get them into trouble with the authorities. They achieve gratification by dominating and humiliating others. These people never form an allegiance with anyone and so move from person to person with remarkable ease. They are alien to emotional attachments and do not feel the slightest remorse on ending an auspicious relationship. The people they leave crumpled in their wake are very adversely affected, as the narcissist is usually very charming. These narcissists are exceptionally dangerous because, for them, truth is only relative. They are masters of manipulation and deceit. They are very adept at scheming beneath a polite and civil veneer. Their plans are usually very cunning and worthy of admiration even though the means is hardly justified. They show no concern for other people's welfare, have no morals, scruples, and are highly deceptive when they deal with others. They will give off an air of arrogance and are driven by a need to get the better of everyone, to prove that they are smarter than everyone. This kind of narcissist may be found in prisons or drug rehabilitation centers, although there are an awful lot of unprincipled narcissists who never come up against the law. When in the vicinity of an unprincipled narcissist always be sure to keep your guard up. They smell insecurities a mile away and can easily turn you into a scapegoat for their next exploit.

Amorous

Amorous narcissists tend to be erotic or seductive in nature, and they measure their entire self-worth around their sometimes many sexual conquests. Their relationships are often pathological and, as soon as they seduce someone, they are likely to throw them to one side while they look for their next conquest. They are never looking for an emotional connection but rather seek to inflate their already bloated ego by sexually dominating other people who they consider as trophies. The victim has more or less no idea that they are being used and sometimes they sincerely fall in love with the narcissists. However, the narcissist genuinely lacks any empathy and will throw them away like paper towels. This makes them outrageous heartbreakers. Not only are they often known as heartbreakers, but they will also do some outrageous things, like pathological lying, conning their sexual partner out of money and other fraudulent acts. They use their sexual prowess to con unsuspecting people. The amorous narcissist is compensating for deep-rooted feelings of inadequacy. In most cases, they get away with it too because people hesitate to complain about them.

Compensatory

Compensatory narcissists are continually looking for a way to compensate for things that happened in the past, perhaps in their childhood, and they do this by creating an illusion that they are superior. They tend to live in a fantasy world where they play the leading role in a theater that doesn't exist rather than living a real life. They imagine achievements in a bid to enhance their self-esteem. They need an audience filled with people who will believe their deceptions, and they are extremely sensitive to how other people perceive them, looking for signs that they are being criticized. They try to compensate for everything that they feel they were deprived off. Their agenda is similar to the other narcissists except that they are more focused rather than being guilty of random acts of narcissism.

Elite

The elite narcissist is, in many ways, very similar to the compensatory narcissist in that they are obsessed with their self-image. The sense of self they create rarely resembles the real person, but they manage to convince themselves and others that they have unique abilities and talents. They will, more often than not, turn a relationship into a contest or a competition where the only goal is to win, to prove to others that they are truly superior. This will happen with any relationship, be it family, work, or love. The elite narcissist is a social climber and will be happy to step on anyone who gets in his or her way. In a way, he is the most dangerous of all the types as he hides in plain sight so effectively that even the ones closest to him perceive him as a good and honest person. An elite narcissist is usually a highly successful businessman or businesswoman who has a very reputable profile. They consider material wealth and assets as a primary objective over real emotion. They are masters of deception and often use their talents to walk over other people. Being as cunning as they get, they usually have a legitimate and reputed business that they use as a front for all of their shady dealings. They are incredibly protective of their personal space. If they get the slightest hint that you are a threat to everything that they have built up, they will eliminate you without a second thought. They are ruthless and without remorse or empathy. They are concerned only with their well being and the achievement of their goals. They will go to any length to achieve what they want.

Below are some of the narcissistic sub-types. These sub-types can be encountered by various people daily. Some can be annoying but tolerated, while some can cause emotional harm.

Conversational

Ever recall an instance where you are talking to a certain person, ranting, or just randomly telling one of your everyday life stories to him? What's unforgettable is how the conversation always manages to end up with him as the subject and the victor? Annoying, right? Not only is it sickening to hear stories with always the same triumphant result, but it is also annoying that they always make you forget what you are about to say due to their constant interruption.

This kind of conversation can happen between normal people as well, but it is almost always the case with people suffering from narcissism. There is an even more aggressive conversational narcissist where they rudely cut you off while you were saying something, so that they can insist their own story whose lead character is always them.

If, by reading this part of the book, you are reminded of that one person who never fails to do this every time you are having a conversation, try to observe. Check out his other mannerisms, habits, or the way he behaves with other people. Chances are, you have a narcissist who is sneakily turning all his friends into his supply sources.

Group Narcissism

Whenever the topic is narcissism, we are always presented with the idea that it is all about a person who cares for nothing else but himself. This is true, but it does not necessarily rule out the possibility of narcissism that can occur in a group.

In group narcissism, the narcissist individual is always a part of the group. Usually, the group is made up of narcissist people who mirror themselves and they don't encounter any problem with having to co-exist with each other. They tend to become the narcissist supply source of each other, and you will know that it is working out as the group acts as a narcissistic entity.

You see, narcissists tend to gather or join each other in groups because it brings them comfort. This is because they are all pretty much similar, and share the same behaviors or habits. There's no questioning about why he behaves this way, and she behaves that way because they all know that they are trying to protect something deep inside them.

Now, this group becomes a protector of the hidden real selves of each member. While this looks nice and beneficial for the narcissist, this does not mean that they are already safe from the danger of self-destruction. It's always there, just below the surface.

Aggressive or Malignant Narcissism

This type of narcissism is your lesser type (like classic, cerebral, somatic, elite, and others) kicked up a notch because it becomes violent and psychopathic. Take Adolf Hitler or Ted Bundy. They can be categorized as aggressive types of narcissists.

Not all narcissists prefer to harm their supply source or victims physically. Most of the time, they just torture or abuse you mentally. However, when a narcissist becomes a bit too physical and performs the murder, the rape, or some other crimes with cold blood, that person can already be categorized as a malignant or aggressive narcissist.

Destructive Narcissism

So we have labels for, pretty much, every type of narcissist out there. Honestly, some psychiatrists do not exactly agree with these labels because identifying a narcissist is more than just knowing all the types and matching the behaviors or signs dominant to that type.

What is more, some narcissists are too clever that they can compensate for some of the behaviors to cover them up. That way, fewer tracks means less disruption to the facade that took them years and so many lies to build and complete.

Some people cannot also be classified as narcissists but they match some of a narcissist's description. Now, why am I saying all these? This is because of this type, the destructive narcissist, is one of those who do not technically fit the definition of a narcissist, but they also inflict pain on themselves and also shows general narcissist patterns.

Out of all the types, the destructive narcissist is the one that seems to be a bit irregular. They have some of the traits that can easily identify them within the various types of the narcissist, and all the while lacks some narcissistic traits that will solidify their being categorized as a narcissist.

Destructive narcissists usually have the most intense characteristics that a narcissist can have. These characteristics will ruin and destroy people around the narcissist, and because of this, you can easily associate them with a pathological narcissist. However, the mentioned characteristics are fewer.

Sexual Narcissism

While this may raise your eyebrows as we have come to know that narcissists aren't exactly crazy about having sex with someone else, let us take a quick look at who these sexual narcissists are. Sex, when blended with grandiosity, becomes sexual narcissism. A sexual narcissist boasts pleasurable sexual skills, has a sexual entitlement, and he also lacks sexual empathy.

The meaning? You get to have intercourse with a sexual narcissist, but as always, it is for his pleasure and not yours. You may feel a satisfaction, and this is no wonder because of the sexual skills of the narcissist. However, if the narcissist feels that he is already satisfied and you aren't yet, even if you are right in the middle of it and he wants to stop, he will stop.

He will only do it with you when he feels like it. So if a sexual narcissist doesn't feel like doing it, even if two weeks have passed already, you will not get any sex.

Another thing that you have to know about sexual narcissists is that they have a big tendency to be an unfaithful partner. Big surprise! Since they feel like they have all the sexual skills, they also feel that they can do it with anyone as long as they are in the mood for it.

Acquired Situational Narcissism (ASN)

This narcissism sub-type is a lot different from the rest of the types, even the main ones, as ASN is acquired later on in life as an adult. All other narcissism types are acquired in the childhood phase of a person's life.

ASN can't just happen to anyone. One needs to have the narcissistic tendency as a child for ASN to be successfully triggered. This type of narcissism is triggered when an adult with a narcissistic tendency suddenly comes across wealth, celebrity-status, or fame. Through this, the previous tendency suddenly blooms into a full-blown narcissistic personality disorder complete with signs, symptoms, behaviors, and more harmful probabilities like the usual type of narcissism. The only difference is the age when the sufferer acquired it.

What feeds their narcissistic cravings are their fans, supporters, people around them, their fake friends, assistants, social media, and the traditional type of media.

Chapter 3: How to Recognize A Narcissistic Mother

> You are not responsible for your mother's happiness (and you never were).

There is a narcissistic personality inventory (NPI) tool based on forced choice questions meant for measuring narcissism in populations of people and a diagnostic tool called the Millon Clinical Multiaxial Inventory (MCMI) used more for individual cases that can be and often are used by medical professionals to diagnose NPD (narcissist personality disorder). These tools can be helpful, but they cannot be used by themselves. They must be used in conjunction with observations of patient behavior. In order to be diagnosed and get treatment for NPD, a patient's condition should meet the criteria for a diagnosis of NPD as defined in the Diagnostic and Statistical Manual of Mental Disorders (DSM-5).

NPD Behavioral Characteristics

The manifestations of narcissist personality disorder are an extreme (some even call it erotic) self-interest that often involves an emphasis on physical appearance. If one is diagnosed with narcissistic personality disorder (NPD), it will generally result as a consequence of a psychiatrist or other qualified health professional observing the patient behaving as if he or she is without the capacity to love anyone but themselves. Most of the time, they are unable to provide their significant other, friends, and other family members with the love, friendship, and caring they all need for a healthy two-way relationship.

Also, the patient exhibits a behavior totally lacking in empathy, disregarding other people's feelings, and ignoring what others in their life care about. They have never "felt anyone else's pain" or even tried to empathize with someone going through a difficult time. In fact, there is only one perspective in the world that exists to the narcissist: their own.

With NPD the narcissist will often have an unrealistic and "out of touch with reality" overconfidence and vanity. They will view their appearance and capabilities as far better than they actually are yet they are unable to deal with even the slightest of criticism. They will hunger for and even demand praise and admiration from those in their life.

Other People Live to Meet the Needs of The Narcissist

Relating to an early paper by Martin Buber referred to earlier in this book, Buber recognized that narcissists view other people as objects to be used for achieving their ends rather than treating people as equal human beings. They will use others to achieve their own ends without the slightest thought of what it may cost the other person.

A Lack of Appropriate Boundaries

This "people are objects to be used" attitude can create a bizarre situation whereby the narcissist cannot distinguish between himself or herself and others. So the narcissist views others as an extension of themselves and think that others exist only to meet their needs. If it turns out that the other people in their life do not exist for this purpose, then the narcissist doesn't even recognize their existence.

That's right! Other people don't even exist in the mind of the narcissist if they are not living to meet every need of the narcissist. This is called the lack of the ability to recognize boundaries. In other words, other people are extensions of themselves and are expected to behave the way the narcissist expects them to and live up to every one of their expectations. There is no boundary between the narcissist and others. For those that the narcissists view as true extensions of themselves, they heap on unwarranted flattery and admiration to maintain the affirmation of their unrealistic and inflated self-worth.

Oblivious

Another behavior of the narcissist is a lack of awareness and insight. They have no idea they have a mental illness and are totally unaware of the impact their behavior has on others. This can make it very difficult to treat narcissists. This also makes it nearly impossible for them to have normal relationships with other people. All of their interaction with the other people in their lives is focused on themselves, making the continuation of any kind of favorable two-way relation that they start extremely difficult for the other person.

Lack of Appropriate Emotion

The narcissist cannot feel appropriate relational emotions because their life is not about others…it's only about them. So not only do they not have normal love emotions, but they also either repress totally or never really feel emotions like regret when they should. After hurting someone else emotionally, even committing acts of violence, when they should feel shame and remorse they do not. They live a life never apologizing, asking for forgiveness or for that matter, even feeling bad about hurting other people emotionally or physically.

Conversely, when someone does something for them that is extraordinary, and a person would normally feel the emotion of gratitude and thank them appropriately, the narcissist will not express gratitude. This is because everyone in the narcissist's life is expected to do wonderful things for the narcissist and it's not "normal" when they don't. In fact, as we will explore next, the emotion that is most likely felt when there is a lack of pandering and admiring the narcissist is injury and rage.

Observing Narcissistic Behavior

Because of the ridiculous self-image the narcissist holds so dearly they will exhibit certain characteristics inherent with the disorder. First of all, they will have a body language that can be called high and mighty, arrogant, conceited, or snooty. They will also be unbelievably overconfident, lie about things they have accomplished that they have not accomplished and pretend to be more important than they obviously are.

All of The Bragging Rights Belong to the Narcissist

They are braggarts to the extreme. Their bragging can be subtle and crafty so as not to be obvious and blatant about it, attempting to avoid getting caught in exaggerations. They can become very good at the "skill" of bragging. The bragging will be determined and unrelenting. If they do have provable achievements, they will always exaggerate the importance of the achievements they can prove. They will always act as if they are an expert at many things even if they do not know the slightest thing about the subject.

The Narcissist Is A Magical Thinker

At times the narcissist will display what you might call magical thinking about just how wonderful they are, what they know, and what they can accomplish. They even will sometimes think that just because they believe something to be correct and true that it is in reality, correct and true, even if there is strong evidence to the contrary. If it is obvious that the narcissist cannot "measure up" to someone else, they will often be envious and show disdain for and disapproval of the person to diminish them as much as possible.

The Entitled Narcissist

According to the narcissist, he or she is entitled to get everything they want and are entitled to have every event in life go their way. They are entitled to the most favorable treatment wherever they go, and everyone needs to comply with their wishes, their way of doing things and their way of thinking. They are always the special person in the relationship and not going along will classify the non-complier as a difficult or dumb and awkward person in the narcissist's special world.

The Manipulating Narcissist

Often times, other people will be forced into a subservient position by way of being an employee, spouse, or child. Alternatively, sometimes the other person will just be timid and afraid to challenge the will and authority of the narcissist. The narcissist will start each new relationship assuming the other person is in a subservient position even when they are not. This puts the narcissist in a position of easily exploiting all who are unfortunate enough to find themselves in this position.

Narcissists of Many Colors

These behaviors and attitudes are what define the mental condition of the narcissist. The condition can assume varying degrees of severity. Some narcissists have such dysfunctional family and social relationships they end up alone, broken and unable to function in society. Others can master manipulation strategies and techniques so well that they become very successful in business or end up at the top of their very demanding professions finally accumulating an "entourage" of subordinates that take care of their every need, pander to their ego, swallow their pride and usually take their very substantial paychecks to the bank. However, narcissists usually fail at one thing in life. They fail at lasting relationships where love defines behavior because they only love themselves. They have a lifelong love affair with themselves and are "forever gazing into the pool at their own reflection".

Chapter 4: Behaviors of a Narcissistic Mother

> **YES, YOU ARE LOVABLE, YOU JUST GAVE YOUR LOVE TO SOMEONE WHO DOESN'T UNDERSTAND LOVE.**

The child with Narcissistic Personality Disorder enters into adulthood with this disorder, which makes forming relationships difficult and impedes satisfaction. They are constantly subjected to internal conflict and always depend psychologically on others. The child is not an object of love that is raised consciously and selflessly; far from it. The child of the narcissistic mother is a mirror by which to gaze at and admire or deplore her.

Narcissistic mothers tend to fall into two basic classifications: smothering mothers and negligent mothers, both of which are discussed in detail below.

Smothering Mothering

The smothering mother, also known as the engulfing mother, cannot determine the boundaries between mother and daughter. The daughter is an appendage of the mother's self in her mind. What is a natural inclination from birth through the toddler stage becomes a problem later when the child is seeking autonomy. It happens surreptitiously, perhaps unconsciously on the part of both actors—mom and daughter. However, the mother does not want to let go; she maneuvers to impede maturity. The proper boundaries are not established, and normal bonding is thus interfered with.

This type of mothering intrudes in the friendships and communications of the growing girl. The girl's private space may be invaded without notice. There are prying questions. The narcissistic engulfing mother also tends to project her own preferences on the daughter, claiming that she really likes this or that type of food or fashion or whatever, rather than the one that the daughter says she likes.

Another negative mothering behavior on the part of the narcissistic-smothered woman is meddling in the daughter's relationships. Typically, she puts down a close friend or husband or schemes to make them unhappy with a view to disrupting a good relationship. She does this out of envy and resentment.

From this behavior mentioned above, the daughter feels pressure not to assert herself and her own tastes and choices. She may not readily stand up to the mother because of the perceived associated risks of anger on the part of the mother or unfair criticisms and other demonstrations of rejection. Should the daughter demand to distance themselves, the mother will persist nonetheless. It could lead to actual stalking and other forms of harassment.

The engulfing type often idealizes her girl in the extreme. Sometimes the daughter is always the reason for the mom's problems and shortcomings. In other cases, she is just plain cold and negligent, absorbed as she is in her own self-admiration and selfishness. Her tactics vary, corresponding to each of these three styles.

To the engulfing mom, there is only the mother. There is no daughter, from her perspective, so the mother assigns herself the right to control and intrude. She may engage in asserting her right as a mother while treating the grown daughter as a little child. She may seek to disturb the balance between relationships by coming between a third person and the daughter (i.e., triangulation).

Others may be fooled. Since the narcissist can be charming and alluring, even charismatic but certainly talkative in the interest of monopolizing the attention in any social circumstances, they may show admiration for the mother-daughter rapport they observe. It can appear to be an ideal relationship, one that is very close rather than pathologically domineering.

From Clinginess to Absence

Next, we proceed to the other end of the spectrum, the mother who ignores the daughter. This kind of mother is so self-absorbed that she has little time or thought for her daughter. Naturally, the impact is quite painful and confusing.

The mother may be physically present most of the time but does not engage with the daughter. She remains withdrawn from the relationship with the daughter and preoccupied with herself and her own activities or ideas. Approaches may only achieve annoyance from this mother. She does not want to listen. She is negligent about the normal duties of parenting: from personal grooming and hygiene, counseling about life, to household organization.

Attempts to raise issues or inquire as to why the mother is so distant get few responses. The reply is more likely to be the cold shoulder or some pretext to move away and refrain from conversation. The reader can well imagine the lack of affection in these circumstances. Any hugging may only be mechanical and tentative on the part of the mother who likes to ignore the child. There are no questions about how the school is going or how the girl is feeling, etc. There are never any compliments. No encouragements. Any conversation likely is conducted with an arrogant or condescending tone.

As the child grows up and carries on her life, there are no phone calls or invitations. Any recognition of a birthday or some other special occasion such as a graduation is addressed nominally, superficially. If any gifts appear, they are according to the mother's own tastes and pushed forward as if the daughter may not be intelligent enough to see its value and suitability, even if the gift is not at all relevant or likable to the younger woman.

Unlike the clingy relationship of the smothering mother, the engulfing, it is easy to remove oneself from the company or attention of the ignoring mom. Regardless, the pain of the emotional and material neglect cuts deep. The daughter can feel unworthy in general as a result. She may not trust other people enough to build close relationships after the experience with this mother. She may feel she never belongs or is unlovable.

Precious Doll or Cause of All Trouble?

It is also important to be aware of the dual danger of the mothers who either imagine a Golden Girl who can do no wrong or the Problem Child who spoils everything. Should a narcissistic mother have two children, she may assign each one of these opposing roles in the family.

Projecting her internal idealization of herself, she exaggerates the attributes and accomplishments of the child she sees as golden. She sits on a privileged and beautiful pedestal above others. This one can never do anything wrong, in her eyes. Any bad behavior or weakness is dismissed while any success or positive feature, no matter how small, is elevated. The narcissistic parent of this one will shower this family member with rewards and support, such as money for clothes, lessons, trips, etc.

Conversely, the scapegoat child is branded the black sheep. All problems of the family, especially those of the mother, are supposedly because of her. This one is placed low on the totem pole, in a dark corner to be spat upon and cursed. Any achievement or positive attribute is squelched or ignored. She is unattractive or even ugly, socially inept, academically stunted, physically repulsive, and so on and so on. She is not worth investing any support in at all.

Should there really be two children forced into taking up opposing functions like this, they no doubt fight and compete. The golden girl has a license to criticize the scapegoat, but the scapegoat child can never win a battle or argument in this household. It is the scapegoat who likely will be punished should friction between them get out of control.

The narcissist certainly does not want to accept that the child labeled the scapegoat is right about anything; nor does she wish to find fault about anything to do with the child given the golden role. Doing either would lead to the narcissist to discover her own weaknesses and mistakes. She does not want to recognize the achievements of the scapegoat child; in fact, that child may be rewarded for failure (e.g., receiving hugs or gifts as signs of love only when something goes wrong).

Indeed, she may be conceived of having something wrong with her, being sick in some way. On the other hand, no recognition of any fault or problem with the golden girl will be made. Her achievements are inflated and over-compensated. She is a healthy one doing well, always. Therefore, the one that is seen as the problem child probably will develop some medical issue such as an eating disorder or depression. The neuroses of the opposite figure are different—perhaps blossoming into a narcissist herself but certainly having anxiety about living up to perfection. There could be other bad habits such as deceit and manipulation so as to help the narcissist mother keep up the façade.

Perhaps, the scapegoat child is the one with the greatest advantage, in the end, however. That's because neglect can drive her to become independent while the smothered child may never be free of the mother's domination, idealization, and control. The latter will have less baggage than the former.

Fathers Who Enable the Narcissistic Mother

What about the narcissistic mother's partner who is the father figure for the daughter? How does he respond? What's his parenting style in the face of his narcissistic spouse?

Unfortunately, in most instances, chances are, he is an enabler. If not the enabler, he probably shares the disorder or has taken off. Should he wish to stick around, how? He would have to support the narcissism.

The father in this type of scenario may be dysfunctional if he too is narcissistic. If he is not, however narcissistic, it is likely that he worships his wife, no matter what, otherwise, the father who is physically present plays along with the defensive narcissistic mom. Out of fear, he adopts the position of the sidekick to echo and assist. He becomes passive and lets the narcissism play out, despite the harm to the daughter, himself, and the woman.

He may become the guy who does the dirty work of attacking the daughter so that the mother can always appear correct, the enforcer deployed to either keep the daughter subjugated to the mother or prevent rebellion. He may rationalize the mother's wrong words and actions. If his partner gets angry, he follows suit or defends her with even greater rage. He may accuse the daughter of being a problem, endeavoring to make her feel ashamed or guilty, should she protest her treatment and desire her freedom and respect.

In most instances, the relationship between the narcissistic mother and the father is one of co-dependency, not love. The father may be anxious about maintaining the structure imposed by the mother and fear change or instability, so he entrenches himself in the accepting attitude and sets himself up as the prop onto which his leading star can lean.

Bloodsucking

The narcissistic woman, with her inflated sense of self and hypersensitivity to problems and criticism, may thrive on drama. The ignoring narcissist tends to make a big deal of the events in their lives and the effects on their emotional state while paying no heed to or suppressing the daughter's ups and downs. This parent is not interested in the disappointments, joys and exciting episodes of her own daughter's life; rather she makes the most of her own.

Everything is supposed to revolve around her. She may even dramatize the experience of others—neighbors, other family members, co-workers or business associates—so as to counter-pose them to her child's experience and try to make her child's life seem smaller. The smothering mother may tell the daughter she is just being a baby when the daughter mentions some trouble or goes through a defeat or disappointment. She may use the daughter's experience to underline the necessity of the daughter remaining under the wing of the engulfing mother, turning it into a justification for not spreading her wings to venture outside of the relationship.

Narcissistic mothers are like a vampire because they prey on the suffering of other people around them. She might display pleasure at passing on bad news for her child. She may exaggerate the misfortunes of others and their consequences and attach causes such as a person (here the child's) inabilities, unluckiness or deficiencies. Think of it—a miscarriage, a break-up, a rejection from a study program—the mother blames the daughter for these saddening and unfortunate events. This parent would most certainly deny any responsibility were there any that lead to disappointment.

Even at a funeral, the narcissist wants to make herself the focus of attention. She interprets what is happening as being related to her. For example, she may imagine that she was specially invited to attend because of her importance, not out of a duty to pay respect and express condolences. She may go on about how drastically the death hit her, not the tragedy it may mean for the deceased person and their loved ones.

Accusations that this woman is thriving on the tragedies of others would be stymied. They would hit a brick wall. Well, denial is a hallmark of many disorders, no?

Chapter 5: The Signs That You Have a Narcissistic Mother

> **THOSE WHO SAY IT COSTS NOTHING TO BE KIND, HAVEN'T MET A NARCISSIST.**

It is sometimes hard to know when we are dealing with a narcissist or not. They are going to be found amongst us, but figuring out the difference between someone who is maybe just a bit of a jerk, someone with a good sense of confidence, and someone who is a narcissist can be difficult. There are a number of symptoms and behaviors that you need to look for in order to determine if you are dealing with someone who is a narcissist or not. Some of the signs that you can watch out for include:

A sense of entitlement and superiority

When the narcissist looks at the world, they see that it is in black and white. Everything is either good or bad, right or wrong, and there is no in-between. With the narcissist, there is a hierarchy in the world, and the narcissist likes to put themselves right at the top. This is really the only place where the narcissist is going to feel like they are safe. The narcissists, at least in their own minds, have to be the best, the most competent, and the most right. Everything needs to be done their way, and they are the ones who have to be in control.

What is interesting here is that often, the narcissist is able to get the superior feeling that they want by being the worst out of the situation. They can be the most injured, the most upset, and the most ill for some time. This is done because it allows the narcissist to feel like they are entitled to receive concern from others, and it even allows them to hurt or demand apologies from others so that they can make things even.

A huge need for validation and attention

Narcissists are going to always need a lot of attention. They need it on a constant basis. These are the people who will follow their victim around the house, asking the other person to find things for them (even though they are perfectly capable of doing it on their own), and saying anything that is going to grab your attention. Even then, this doesn't seem to be enough for the narcissist.

When we look at the need for validation by the narcissist, it is like a funnel. You can pour in a lot of supportive and positive words; it seems like they just flow right through the narcissist and don't stick. You can spend all day telling the narcissist that you approve of them, admire them, and love them, and it is never going to be enough for them. Moreover, this is because most narcissists believe that deep down, no one can really love them. Despite their bragging and grand behavior, the narcissist is going to be insecure, and they have a big fear of not being able to measure up to others.

They need to be in control

Since narcissists are always going to be disappointed in the way that life unfolds around them, they are going to do what they can to try and control it, to see if they are able to mold it in some way to their liking

In the mind of the narcissist, there is going to be a story line about what each character in a specific interaction should be doing and saying. Of course, the real world doesn't follow this story line. and when that happens, the narcissist is going to feel upset about it. They will get mad and try to control the situation to their own liking.

They like to blame and deflect

Even though the narcissist is going to insist that they are the ones who are in control, they are never going to be responsible for any negative results. If the results of their control are good, they will jump right in and expect all of the praise and adoration that they think they deserve. However, if things don't fall into place or things don't go according to the plan that they had, then the narcissist will refuse to take the blame. There is always someone else to blame for the situation, and the narcissist will take advantage of this.

Sometimes the blame is going to be a bit more generalized. They may say things like all students, all bosses, all police and so on. Alternatively, the narcissist may pick one person to blame for the situation. However, you may find that the narcissist is more likely to blame whoever is the most emotionally close to them, the one who is the most loving, loyal, and attached to them. In order to make sure that they always look perfect, the narcissist will always be able to find someone else to blame for things that go wrong.

Lack of boundaries

When it comes to knowing a narcissist, you may notice that they are not able to accurately see where they end and where another person begins. They think in a similar way to how a two-year-old would act, that everything belongs to them, that everyone else must feel and think the same way as they do, and that everyone, no matter who, wants the same things that they do.

What comes next is a lot of insult and shock when the narcissist finds out that someone is going to tell them no. If the narcissist wants to get something from another person, they are going to go through great lengths in order to figure out how to get it. They will use a lot of different techniques, including pouting, rejecting, demanding, cajoling, and persistence.

Lack of empathy

Narcissists are going to have very little ability when it comes to empathizing with others. They are going to be very self-involved and selfish, and they are going to run into trouble when it comes to an understanding of the way that others are going to feel. They think that everyone else is the same as them, and they don't really take the time to think about how others are going to feel. It is unlikely that you are going to find one who is truly guilty, remorseful, or apologetic in any way.

However, on the other end of things, the narcissist is going to be really attuned to any rejection, anger, and threat that they perceive from others. At the same time, they are going to be pretty much blind to the feelings of others around them. They can misread even the smallest of facial expressions, and they are going to be biased to thinking that all facial expressions are going to be negative. Moreover, unless you decide to act out these emotions in a theatrical manner, it is impossible for the narcissist to perceive what you are feeling.

Another issue that can come up is if your expressions and your words are not congruent, then the narcissist will respond erroneously. This is why it is common a narcissist is more likely to misinterpret sarcasm as an actual agreement or joking as a personal attack. Their lack of ability to read body language is one of the reasons that a narcissist is going to have trouble being empathetic to your feelings. They aren't going to see them, they aren't going to interpret the emotions right, and they pretty much assume that everyone else thinks the same way that they do.

Another thing to consider is that narcissists are going to lack an understanding of the nature of feelings. They don't really understand how or why feelings occur.

They assume that feelings are going to happen outside of them, rather than something that is internal. They think that you are the one who causes their feelings, especially when it comes to the negative ones. They assume that because you aren't following along with their plan, or because they are feeling vulnerable around you, that you are the one to blame.

Emotional reasoning

It is likely that at some point, you have made the mistake of trying to use logic and reason with a narcissist in the hopes of trying to get them to understand the effect they are having on you. You think that if you talk about this, they will understand the way that this behavior is hurting you and that they will change. However, these kinds of explanations are not going to make much sense at all to the narcissist, because they are really only aware of their own feelings and thoughts. They may say that they understand up and down, but they really don't.

Because of this, narcissists are going to make decisions about how they feel about something. For example, if they like the way that they feel when they drive it, they will go out and have a red sports car. It doesn't matter if it is going to work in their budget or for their family.

Splitting

The personality of a narcissist is going to be split into both bad and good parts, and they are going to split up the things in their relationships as well. Any of the negative behaviors or thoughts that come up are going to be blamed on either the victim or other people. The narcissist is going to deny that they said any negative words, or did anything negative in terms of actions, while still accusing and disapproving of their partner. When they look back at things, they are going to remember them as either completely good or really horrible. There isn't a way for them to mix together these two things.

For example, have you ever gone on a vacation with someone who said that the whole thing was ruined because there was one bad day in terms of weather, or the reservation for the hotel vacation didn't meet their expectations? A narcissist isn't able to see, feel, or remember both the negative and the positive that came in the situation. They are able to just deal with one perspective at a time, and that perspective is going to be their own.

Anxiety

Another thing that you are going to notice with a lot of narcissists is that they are going to feel a lot of anxiety about what is going on in their lives. Some narcissists are going to show their anxiety by talking all the time about the doom that they think is about to happen, while there are others who are more likely to hide and then repress their anxiety.

For the most part, you will notice that a narcissist is going to project their anxiety onto the ones they love. They are willing to accuse the ones they love of being mentally ill, being unsupportive, of being negative, of being selfish, and of not responding to the needs of the narcissist. The reason that they do this is because it transfers some of the anxiety to the loved one, in the hopes that they, the narcissist, will not feel the pain at all. As the victim starts to feel worse and worse, the narcissist is able to make themselves feel better. In fact, this is a good way for the narcissist to start to feel stronger and like they are the superior one in the situation.

Shame

It is uncommon for a narcissist to feel a lot of guilt, simply because they think that they are the ones who are always right. Moreover, they don't have any idea that their behaviors are really having a negative effect on others. However, a narcissist is indeed going to feel a lot of shame. Shame, in this case, is going to be the belief that there is something either personally wrong or bad about who you are. Moreover, the narcissist is not going to like this at all.

Buried in a deep part of the narcissist, which they are going to repress quite a bit, are a bunch of insecurities, rejected traits, and fears. Moreover, the narcissist is going to keep these hidden so that others are not able to see them, even the narcissist. It is common for the narcissist to reject these feelings and thoughts because they are really ashamed of even feeling them at all.

Trouble communicating at work or inability to work as part of a team

Thoughtful and cooperative behaviors are going to require each person to understand the thoughts and feelings of another person. How is the other person going to feel when you act or say a certain thing? Will this action be one that is going to make you both happy? Is this action, or are these words going to make a change in your relationship?

These are questions that a normal person is going to ask when it comes to working with a team. But these are questions that a narcissist is going to have no motivation or capacity to think about. You should never expect that the narcissist is going to understand your feelings, they are not going to give up anything, and they will not give in just for the benefit of someone else. It will be useless to try.

Because of this, it is hard to work with a narcissist. They do not understand how others feel, and they have no want to learn how to do this either. So they are less likely to get along. They won't give in, they won't admit when they are wrong, but they will certainly take all of the credit when things start going well. They are really hard to work with and can make the whole team feel frustrated.

As you can see, a lot of the traits that come with being a narcissist are going to make it difficult for them to get along in society and do well. They are not able to understand the way that normal people are going to think, and they are much more interested in making sure that they are the ones who are in charge, and that they are the ones that get what they need. This can make it a challenge for them to get along well with others.

Then there could be an issue with parents who are too neglectful. This is going to cause the child to overcompensate, hiding all of the negative things that their parents didn't like about them when they were younger, and just trying to show off an image that is perfect to the world. Whether the neglect was intentional or not didn't matter, the individual may have learned how to just showcase their positive attributes as a way to make themselves look better and gain approval from the outside world.

Another cause that could bring out narcissism in an individual is if their parent, one or both, were narcissists. They would have learned this kind of behavior from their parent as they are growing up, and it is likely that they are going to exhibit the same kinds of personality traits as well.

Many people also worry about the connected world that we have right now. They worry that because the world is spending so much time on social media and online, rather than getting out there and making real connections with those around them, that narcissism is going to become a bigger problem in the future. People spend so much time alone without the help or interaction of others, and they spend so much time trying to show their best side online that it is no wonder that many of them are going to struggle when it comes to having narcissistic personality disorder.

Right now, many of the studies that have been done on this condition have not found a ton of therapies and treatments to help with this condition. Many times the narcissist doesn't see a problem, so they don't want to work on making that problem any better. Right now, the most common treatments to work with will be therapy, either group therapy or individual therapy.

If you have been around someone who has NPD and who is a narcissist, you will notice that they are going to have very little care for others. They are going to want to spend their time worrying about their own goals and needs, rather than the goals and needs of others. They have no empathy for others, and they assume that everyone else must feel and think in the same manner that they do.

These people feed on constant praise. Whether they are at work, at school, or in a relationship, they demand that the other person feeds into their need for love and attention all of the time. Also, they often need to be the best, the strongest, and the one who is the most right at all times.

When it comes to a relationship, this can be really harmful to the other partner. In order to keep the partner in place and to stay in that relationship, and to ensure that they are able to get a constant amount of love and attention, the narcissist is going to work to put their partner down. They will be the one in control, and the other person will feel like they have to depend and rely on the narcissist at all times.

When it comes to working, the narcissist is able to take control as well. They do well at being a boss because they do have a lot of the great characteristics that come with being the leader. However, they are also going to miss out on some of the ones that are needed as well. Narcissists like to be in control, but they will often take credit for all of the good things that happen in the business or with a project, even if they have nothing to do with it.

It is not uncommon for a narcissist to be the reason that a company starts to have some problems as well. The narcissist is not able to take any blame for anything that happens in the company. And they can never admit when they were the ones who were wrong. Because of this, they are going to keep going with poor decisions, and blaming other people, rather than taking care of the situation when it comes up.

Dealing with a narcissist can be hard. They refuse to admit when they are the ones who are wrong, and their main goal is to make themselves look good, and feed themselves a lot of attention and focus from others. And since they don't really understand the needs and wants of others, there comes an even bigger challenge to talk with them, to work with them, and many times being in a relationship, being related to them, and working with them can feel like a major headache to a lot of people.

Why do some people become a narcissist?

There are a lot of theories out there when it comes to why someone may be considered a narcissist. Many times those who are narcissistic turned out that way because they had parents who are narcissistic. In some cases, the child was neglected because the parents were busy, they got sick, or they were so focused on themselves (if they were a narcissist) that they were not able to pay attention to their child at all. But then there are times when the parents may have been too overindulgent and not able to let the child fail, or ever notice when something bad happened with that child. They only focused on the good.

Either way, the child was either told that they were all bad and they hid some of those bad traits about themselves, or they were all good, and they just won't admit that there are some negative traits that they should be aware of. This can lead to the narcissist hiding the bad, and only focusing on the good, exaggerating it to a point where they think that they are the best person around.

When you meet with someone who is a narcissist, you will notice that their levels of self-esteem are going to be inflated. They are going to be very fragile because of this, usually because the flip side of this self-aggrandized feeling leaves them with low self-esteem. So, because their self-esteem is so low, no matter how much others are going to praise them and try to bring them up, this person is going to react badly to any kind of criticism.

Being condescending is going to be another common dynamic that is found in a narcissistic relationship. Often this is a behavior that is going to be traced back to the need, a very desperate need, that narcissists have to be liked, adored, and above others.

Are there different types of narcissism to watch out for?

While it is common for all narcissists to show certain types of behaviors, you will realize quickly that not all of them are going to be the same. There are actually two broad types of narcissism that are recognized in our world today, including the vulnerable narcissism and the grandiose narcissism. These are going to be two different types of the same problem, and they are going to stem from different early childhood experiences and are going to lead to some different behaviors in a relationship.

Let's take a look at how each one is going to work. When you interact with a grandiose narcissist, you will notice that they show off a lot of dominance, aggression, and grandiosity. They are going to be less sensitive to what others say and usually a lot more confident in the process as well. You may find that these individuals are elitists, and they have no problem when it is time to tell everyone how great they are.

These narcissists want to be treated in this superior manner because they were treated that way as a child. And now that they are progressing through life, they still expect to get this kind of treatment from others. When we look at how this kind of behavior is going to influence a relationship, the grandiose narcissist is more likely to be unfaithful, and even to leave the other partner quickly if they feel that they are no longer getting that special treatment that they have come to know and expect.

Then there are the vulnerable narcissists. These individuals are going to be a bit more sensitive when we talk about emotions. They are going to have a kind of fragile grandiosity, where their narcissism is going to serve as a type of façade protecting some of their deeper feelings of incompetence and inadequacy.

You may find that these narcissists are going to go back and forth between feeling inferior and superior. They are going to feel like they are the victim most of the time, and they will be anxious any time that they think they are not getting the special treatment that they want.

When it comes to this kind of narcissism, it is going to show up early in childhood, and it is a good way for the individual to deal with any of the neglect and the abuse that they had to deal with on a regular basis. When they are in a relationship, the narcissist is going to worry quite a bit about how their partners will perceive them. In addition, this kind of narcissist is going to be paranoid, jealous, and possessive about their partners and will not want those partners to leave their sight because of these issues.

Chapter 6: Treatment for Children of Narcissistic Mothers

> stop reconnecting with toxic people from your past because you're lonely. focus on getting better and attracting better

There are links between narcissistic parenting and the symptoms of self-blame and low self-esteem experienced and demonstrated by the children who have suffered narcissistic parenting. In 2004, Guile, Mbekou, and Lageix published the results of a clinical study of narcissistic youths and youths who had narcissistic parents. They were particularly interested in the responses of such parents and youths to therapy.

The study group consisted of 36 children from ages nine to 13. They were all in therapeutic programs with parental counseling and psychodynamic psychotherapy. They were assessed for narcissism and their attitude and use of psychology and social services.

The study revealed that children and parents assessed with narcissism were resistant to psychosocial services that offered treatment and support. They were less likely to take advantage of such treatment and support precisely because of narcissistic assumptions, biases, and emotionality. Child victims of narcissistic parenting tend to blame themselves and feel inferior, while the narcissistic child devalues other people, denies their issues, wants to avoid feeling vulnerable, and lacks motivation.

The Relevance of Self-Help

When it comes to moving past the issues created by a narcissistic mother, professional help is almost always recommended. Nevertheless, the individual could begin some mental processes to check their own problematic thoughts, emotions, and actions that arise from the effects of incorrect parenting. The main thing is to recognize that the parent has a mental health problem. Then she can identify some symptoms that the parent exhibits and narrow down the possible disorders.

It may well be that the parent suffers from more than one and also signals parallel conditions such as hypersexuality, anxiety issues, or substance abuse. Committed to researching what might be the ailments, the child of the narcissistic parent will come across narcissism and recognize it. Once she does, she can identify some of the symptoms of narcissism, which nurtures an understanding of the disorder.

There is no point in denial. Though a defense mechanism itself, denial blocks the path to the processes of understanding and committing to change the responses and the relationship. Neither is clinging to hope that the parent will love and take responsibility. This false hope is self-defeating.

This admission and acceptance may make it easier for the affected daughter to feel compassion for themselves and to gain comprehension of her own feelings, behaviors, and ideas. She can start to relate them to negative parenting. She can overcome anger at the parent for the lack of love when she sees that the parent has a serious problem, which is the parent's issue and not theirs — seeing the associations can empower the person and motivate them to seek assistance and make some changes. An important thing to understand is the lack of empathy. Also, it should be understood that this state of a person comes from a weak sense of self, lack of self-love and over-sensitivity or defensiveness on the part of the parent. The child of the narcissist may allow herself to detach from and reset the faulty relationship with the parent.

It is likely that the daughter of such a parent will be depressed. It will be important to recognize this and get treatment for depression. The person should come to understand that it is a normal response to abuse and lack of parental emotional nurturing. It is possible for the individual to understand, get over it, and move on in life. There is no point in attempting to fix it, and the past cannot be undone. As already stated above, the narcissist does not like to be challenged.

If there is a second parent present, concentrate energies and efforts in that direction. The child can be an enabler, assisting the second parent in asserting themselves, rejecting narcissistic behavior, and helping the parent to let go. The child can challenge the co-narcissist or narcissism enabler to become aware of their role and the effects it has had on the offspring. She can also stand up to and resist that parent's defense and justification for the narcissist. By winning him over to her side, a united front against the harmful parent can be established.

Furthermore, it is helpful for the child of a narcissist to know and appreciate the family roles and dynamics and her own place on the web. She can find out whether she falls into a category of golden girl or scapegoat. It can help foster understanding of the alienation from other family members and their own clinginess or dejection. It can make someone see how they may be serving narcissism or being manipulated and controlled by narcissism.

In addition, the person will have to draw boundaries. Aware of any behaviors that amount to fueling narcissism or being subjugated by it, the individual can begin to give up compliance and subservience. She can set up her own rules. Most importantly, she can learn to admit and act on her wants and feelings. She can adjust their identity and emotions. By this point, the process of renegotiating the relationship and separating oneself from narcissistic processes get hard. It takes quite a bit of time.

Understand your vulnerability and why narcissists may target someone. Identify other narcissists and stay away from them. Remove the stingers and needles they have assaulted you with. Do not let them contaminate and infect you. There is no need to blame oneself for what the parent is responsible for. Let go of blame and feel compassion for yourself and circumstances. Do not punish yourself anymore. Do not keep dragging yourself down. Get on with your own responsibility of living your own life and living with respect and dignity.

At the same time, it is important to acknowledge one's own feelings about the narcissistic parent. Do not judge. It is okay to feel compassion for the parent diagnosed with NPD. It is okay to reserve some love for that person. There could be ways of supporting the person if they admit to a problem and seek help. The child can be a catalyst for making treatment happen and keeping it up.

Explore the family history and understand the processes that have occurred and the roles and dynamics of the family led by a narcissist. Then, it is healthy to let oneself feel the pain from the bad experiences and the lack of nurturing. After that, gain some appreciation for signs of personal growth and life accomplishments despite the poor parenting and lack of familial support. The person should feel good about real assets and achievements.

Follow up that process by getting back out into the world on a quest to find new relationships or make relationships more functional wherever possible (probably not the relationship with the narcissist parent, but perhaps with siblings, the other parent and other relatives, friends, business and work associates). Overall, the efforts aimed at healing should be to arrive at a firmer and more confident sense of the self.

Next is the business of setting the boundary. The woman should let the mother know when she is intruding and violating her rights and duties as the mother of an adult. She should assert herself and stand up to the problem behavior that interferes and violates respect for her, no matter the antics and retaliations exhibited by that mother.

The main purpose is not to change the relationship with the mother (or narcissistic father); it is actually to change the relationship with the anxiety associated with the mother-daughter dynamic and the bad feelings it generates.

Therapy

Speaking of professional therapeutic options, the adult must first accept there is a problem, then look back at childhood and accept the reality of it. This takes abandoning fantasies about childhood. The person must be ready and equipped to be responsible for making a change. They have to account for the problem behavior and causal factors.

The five-stage therapeutic process of recovery includes the following. First is recalling and discussing experiences as a child. The childhood events are reconstrued in a more realistic way and the fantasies identified and rejected. Next, the person will feel sad about losing the fantasy because a way of thinking and behaving has been built around it. Also, the reality will no doubt be disappointing and sad. The foreseen benefit, however, is that the person no longer relies on hope based on the fantasies.

In the third phase, the narcissistic family and its symptoms and outcomes are appreciated and recognized. Considering herself in the present, the therapist and the client work together to sort out the positive thoughts, feelings, and behaviors from the negative ones, deciding which to keep and which to let go. The final stage necessary to pass through for recovery is making the commitment to change. The aim is to become more socially functional for success in areas of life, such as relationships, career, household organization, and inner happiness.

To clarify the process of initiating and carrying through with the change, it is necessary to articulate certain problematic behaviors that inhibit healthy functioning, starting with assertiveness. Because of the immersion in the life of a narcissistic family, the child growing up there may not know what they think and feel. There may be long buried sentiments. It will then be appropriate to learn communication skills especially to express feelings by means of certain techniques. The client thereby becomes more aware of what they think and feel and better skilled at conveying what they think and want. Functioning improves because the person can learn to say aloud what they prefer or expect or feel instead of walking away or getting angry.

Another area that needs work is by establishing boundaries. The offspring of narcissistic parenting may be reluctant to draw boundaries (between themselves and others, between their own likes and wants and those of others) because they do not wish to disappoint. Setting boundaries enables the person to take more control. Also, she learns to accept criticism and make it through disapproval.

Tips for defining boundaries include:

1.   You are able to express your needs to others, although you cannot always get what you need from others.

2.   How you feel is a reality. It is just what you feel and does not need to be rationalized.

3.   Asserting your thoughts and feelings does not have to be destructive or hurtful. You can learn to articulate them effectively in an appropriate way.

Different experts offer different interpretations and recommendations for therapy and action to overcome the pain and correct poorly functioning thoughts and behaviors stemming from the experience of surviving a narcissistic parent. Most available treatments are for adults.

The chief issue with respect to therapy is self-worth and self-respect. This devaluation of the self may even be a result of rejecting narcissistic behavior and an effort to avoid behaving like a narcissistic person. They counter the fear of developing narcissism by under-valuing themselves.

To improve self-esteem, the offspring of the narcissistic parent will have to retrace the history of their childhood. The parents probably will not offer any help. In fact, they could be a hindrance to the process by reconstructing the past to suit them. Part of the reason is their own condition of coldness and self-centeredness. That is precisely why intervention by a professional therapist is vital.

The client will probably need to shed any belief that the narcissistic parent has empathy and is interested in correcting things. She will not likely accept the revised version of the past and the truth of the relationship with her. Compassion for oneself and distance from the parenting is bound to aid the person to recover. It is possible that big results can happen through professional therapy for the person who has suffered under the shadow of a narcissistic parent.

Cognitive Behavioral Therapy (CBT)

Cognitive Behavioral Therapy (CBT) is a type of therapy that focuses on analyzing why a person feels the way they do based on the unique ways they view specific scenarios. As a variety of mental health issues are based on distorted ways of looking at the world, CBT is effective because it shows patients the error of their thoughts.

Cognitive Behavioural Therapy functions around a handful of core beliefs, starting with the fact that thoughts lead directly to actions and can also influence behaviors. This is usually represented on a diagram in a cycle. It illustrates that if we can change one component of the cycle, then we can change all three. It also shows how these things are all interconnected rather than independent of each other.

The second concept is especially important as it relates to anxiety (even though CBT can treat many forms of mental illness). Anxiety's non-stop obsession with what can be makes us feel like we've lost control over our lives and everything around us. However, that isn't the problem. The problem is that it tries to make us take control of everything to protect ourselves. CBT teaches us to accept what's beyond our control and to recognize and hold on to what is. This is largely done through introspection.

CBT works on the assumption that thoughts, behaviors, and feelings are all constantly interacting and influencing each other. Thus, the way a person thinks or interprets a given situation will ultimately determine how they feel about it and thus, how they will react to it.

For example, consider a pair of individuals who both recently failed to do as well as they would like on a difficult and important test. The first person thinks that if they were smarter, they would have done better on the test, which must mean that they are stupid. They feel anxious about the idea of future tests and depressed about their prospects for the class overall. As a result, they develop a negative opinion of themselves while at the same time not taking any positive actions when it comes to improving how they prepare for future tests as they now believe that their lack of basic intelligence is the root of the problem.

The other person, on the contrary, decides that the only reason they did poorly on the test was that they didn't study enough as they thought they already knew the material. While this will lead to feelings of disappointment in the short-term, it will also make it possible for them to feel better about the next test they have. What's more, it also leads to more productive behavior in the future as they can more readily ensure that the same thing doesn't happen next time by studying more thoroughly in the future.

What really distinguishes Cognitive Behavioural Therapy apart from the other kinds of therapies is the fact that it is structured around completing two separate, distinct tasks, which are Cognitive Restructuring and Behavioral Activation.

Cognitive Behavioural Therapy also places most of its focus on the present by bringing out the way the patient feels in the moment rather than the underlying reasons the patient might feel a specific way.

Cognitive Behavioural Therapy is also known for its focus on specific problems the patient might be facing rather than the more general picture of all issues or the patient's overall mental state.

In either group or individual sessions of the CBT, problem thinking and behavior will be identified first, then prioritized and then finally addressed in order of necessity.

CBT is primarily education-based, which means that the therapist is going to use structured learning experiences as a way for patients to learn to monitor the negative thoughts and images that come into their minds. The goal, then, is to recognize how these contradictory ideas affect the physical condition and behavior and to understand how these things affect mood.

It is also important to note that CBT patients are generally expected to take an active role in their therapy experience as well. This means they are going to be regularly given homework assignments after each therapy session, some of which will even be graded. These assignments will be reviewed at the beginning of each session. During sessions, a wide variety of different strategies are going to be used, including things like behavioral experiments, guided discovery, imagery, role-playing, Socratic questioning, and more. Despite this, CBT sessions are typically limited in nature, rarely lasting more than four months.

While each of the exercises discussed in the following chapters is going to be more effective for treating some issues than others, this doesn't necessarily mean you are going to find something to deal with your specific issues here.

To determine if Cognitive Behavioural Therapy is a good fit for you, there are some questions you can ask yourself:

Do you prefer focusing on your current problems as opposed to those from the past?

Do you believe that talking about your current troubles is more useful than discussing childhood experiences?

Do you consider yourself to be primarily focused on achieving your goals in as short of a period as possible?

Do you prefer therapy sessions where the therapist is active instead of just a passive recipient?

Do you prefer structured therapy sessions over those that are open-ended?

Do you feel willing to put in effort on your own to support your therapy?

If you answered yes to a majority of these questions, then CBT is likely going to be effective when it comes to helping you reach your goals. While there are some exercises you will be able to successfully complete by yourself; you will find that you are far more successful with the help of a professional as opposed to going it alone. Additionally, if you are dealing with any issues that may be life-threatening, it is recommended that you seek professional help as soon as possible to ensure you don't become a danger to yourself and others.

Neurological Relief

Eye Movement Desensitization and Reprocessing Therapy (EMDRT)

Brain scans can show patients the condition of the hippocampus (short-term memory bank at the rear of the brain). The hippocampus can be stimulated to regrow, and EMDR is a great place to start. Eye Movement Desensitization and Reprocessing Therapy (EMDRT) is one proven effective brain therapy. At least one research study indicates that the hippocampus of PTSD patients can grow back as much as six percent by the implementation of EMDR. This technique works on soothing the excessive stimulation of the amygdala, the center of basic emotions such as fear.

EMDRT results tend to be visible fairly quickly with over 30 controlled studies in the past decade finding that victims of a single trauma were able to see measurable improvements after 270 minutes of treatment spread out across three sessions. This efficacy is improved to 100 percent among single-trauma cases and 70 percent in multi-trauma scenarios when treatment is instead spread out over six sessions.

EMDRT works using a highly structured process that looks at not just the present but the past and future ramifications of stressful and negative memories as well. These steps are detailed below and should only be performed by those trained explicitly in EMDRT as it can do more harm than good when performed incorrectly.

EMDRT steps

1. Planning (Treatment and History): This step is relatively standard and includes an evaluation and a detailed history of the issue in question. Unlike some CBT variants, EMDRT is very interested in the client's past, specifically, distressing memories which are then tagged as targets of reprocessing. EMDRT is typically focused primarily on the most significant and most difficult experiences the client has been through as changing those will then cause the most noticeable change overall.

2. Learn to relax: An essential aspect of EMDRT is staying calm between sessions before learning to direct your eye movements yourself. Because of this, therapists suggest and help practice various relaxation techniques, including guided imagery before getting into actual EMDRT techniques. Another particularly useful relaxation technique that can aid in EMDRT is mindfulness meditation.

3. VOC Scale: The VOC scale, otherwise known as the Validity of Cognition scale is what is used to calibrate a person who is going to be using EMDRT for the first time. Initially, the patient will be asked to think of a specific image that you can relate negatively to, before then doing the same thing with a positive image instead. The patient will then be asked to consider how completely they believe in the positive image, followed by the negative image. They will then be asked to list any feelings that the images might generate as well as their overall level of intensity. They will finally be asked to link those sensations with various parts of the body, if relevant.

4. Reprocessing: The reprocessing step of EMDRT focuses on retraining the brain to experience positive emotions as opposed to the negative ones that are currently associated with specific memories. As a part of this exercise, the client will focus on trouble spots for about a minute at a time. While doing so, they will also be asked to focus on something that will cause them to look either left or right, as opposed to in the way that is currently associated with the negative memory in question.

The nature of the added stimulus isn't important; what is important is that it remains in play long enough for the eye movement to be moved away from the trouble spot. During each session, the patient's eyes will be moved further and further from the trouble spot, improving their reaction to it in the process.

5. Improve beliefs: Once reprocessing has occurred a few times, the next step will be for the patient to retain the new patterns by relating back to the positive thoughts they generated earlier. This part of the process will also include another round of the stimulus from the previous step to ensure that future negative memories create the same mitigated response. During this step, the patient must focus on each part of the new emotion, including how it makes them feel both mentally and physically. After they have a firm grasp on the emotion, they will then be instructed to think about it in conjunction with the stimuli in question with enough conviction that the two become interconnected in your mind.

Being mindful is a process of existing entirely at the moment using the information your senses are providing you as an anchor to prevent you from interacting with the thoughts that are racing through your head. The goal is to notice thoughts without interacting with them, and it can make avoiding negative thoughts before they lead to panic and anxiety easier than you may have ever thought possible. It can be practiced anywhere at any time, all you have to do is focus on breathing deeply and the physical sensations that doing so creates throughout your body.

The Treatment of Children suffering from NPD

A psychiatrist should talk to the child to examine how they see themselves. How much self-love and self-importance does she express? How is school going? Are there friends? A variety of assessment tools could be implemented. The doctor might decide to make use of forms such as questionnaires, and there may be tests according to scales.

When the therapist is introduced, the attitude displayed, and manner of interacting in response to the intervention is also looked at. There should be a full physical examination to determine whether other causes are at play.

Ruling out physical causes, psychoanalytic inquiry seeks to find out whether other disorders are presented. There could be depression, high anxiety or a coinciding second personality disorder.

Once it is determined the child has NPD, the extent of the disorder is measured. Is it mild, moderate, or severe? Is it based on moods only? Finally, a plan for caring for the mental health of the child is sketched out. Therapy may address recovery or, based on a diagnosis that the condition and its situation are highly complex; the goal may be the management of the disorder.

One kind or a range of cognitive behavior therapy (CBT) may be applied. This identifies problematic thoughts, emotions, and behaviors. Most schools of cognitive behavior therapy aim to stop these problems and eradicate or alter them, though the mindfulness and acceptance strain of therapies may aim at making the person aware of the negative inner processes and trying to have the client reset their values. The latter approach wants the client to under-value the negative personal experiences, assuming that they will remain in the background, by placing more value on healthy goals. The relationship to the negative experience is changed to redirect the person's life and help them function better.

Treating the Narcissistic Parent's Inner Child

The narcissist has, in all likelihood, built up a fortress to protect internal pain. The narcissist has her history with hurt and baggage, after all. She creates defense mechanisms to keep from feeling vulnerable or needy. The fear and vulnerability is the inner child.

There are a variety of emotions triggered by sensitivity the narcissist has trouble feeling as they are viewed as threats that could open up the inner pain. They are an aversion to ridicule, insecurity or lack of control, sensing deficiency, lack of emotional nourishment, and abandonment. The narcissist wants to prevent a release of their innermost true feelings and would prefer to keep up the charade. A therapist would perceive the denial or lack of insight about the person's real feelings and experiences; the emotionality would appear stymied or splintered. A big motivation is the covering up of shame for what lies beneath. The person could respond to therapy and learn self-compassion, understanding that it is okay to feel vulnerable. She could be encouraged to let the innermost feelings surface if there are accompanying tactics of self-soothing and a guiding, empathetic therapist.

This process can be successful if the therapist starts out by coaxing the inner child to reveal itself and developing a bond with that inner child. The therapist makes the therapeutic environment safe for the client. The therapist could operate as a role model, suggesting alternative emotional responses. A combination of psycho-education and role modeling can manage to get the client to accept and take on adjusted parenting behaviors and attitudes. This is done through a process of having the client re-parent herself and her wounded insides. Even if the client does not confess to any painful experiences, they could be led through the process anyway.

From there, a recovery plan could be constructed wherein the basic, best parenting behaviors are identified in contrast with the non-functioning or harmful parenting behaviors. Stine characterizes this process as being akin to a treatment for addiction that needs to be mitigated and put aside. The adult learns to abstain from negative behaviors, including behaviors that are passive-aggressive responses, manipulating, blaming, entitling, womanizing, yelling, exiting dramatically, and substance abuse.

The client learns awareness of the need for self-protection and the strategies she uses to protect the inner child. Clients still get to protect themselves. They learn healthier ways of maintaining the self and shielding themselves from hurt and exposure. They learn healthier ways of responding to and interacting with others. In short, they correct themselves by learning how to care for themselves.

The therapist also has to take care of herself, because of the narcissist's tendencies to be abrasive, dependent and needy. Engagement with this type of client can be especially frustrating and draining. The therapist has to demand respect and maintain respect for the client but may need to take breaks and manage her own health during the program of therapy.

Chapter 7: Things Narcissistic Mothers Say for Mental Manipulation and Control

> Sometimes you need to stop seeing the good in people and start seeing what they show you...

To keep you under control, your mother has used different techniques that I'll describe later. Your mother may not have used all of them, and she may have used different techniques at the same time. Toxic mothers are quite predictable and have very similar action patterns. However, they are unique people, and not all use the same torture weapons. You'll recognize them as you read through them.

Reading the abuse techniques will bring you back to your childhood, to painful moments. Please keep your notebook with you. Each technique you read will take your memory to specific moments, stories that you may have buried.

Bringing them to memory again will hurt you. However, please write them down. Believe me, that the exercise of recognizing your pain, its origin, and taking it out will help you. Doing this is going to get you emotional, and will even bring out your emotional defensive behaviors like anger and great sadness. I recommend you that if you live with someone, partner, children, friends, share with them your healing process. You don't want them to worry about seeing you suffer.

But don't worry. I won't allow you to stay in pain. You'll see later that focusing on the pain leaves you chained to it. But to reach the part where you can start to change and heal. First you need to recognize what it's that you have. You need to be aware of every symptom you have.

Let's start seeing the abuse techniques that your mother has used to keep you under her control. Let your tears sprout; you need to clean yourself from pain.

Infantilizes

Infantilizing consists of underestimating physical and mental abilities, which favors a loss of independence and autonomy. This form of abuse translates into isolation and a diminution of the physical, cognitive, functional, and emotional faculties.

Examples of infantilization can be the following:

- Give money constantly to the daughter, reinforcing the message that the daughter can't fend for herself. Logically, the daughter will never know how to survive and seek a life of her own if the mother doesn't let her.

- Approve or disapprove of your friendships; she decides who is good or bad for you.

- Telling you what you should wear.

- Saying you're too young to get married, to leave home, etc. (even if you're 40!)

- Write down how your mother infantilized you when you were younger and how she does it now. Take your time, read the point again if necessary. Go for a walk and let your memories come up.

Invalidation

Invalidating is rejecting, ignoring, ridiculing, mocking, judging or diminishing someone's feelings. The toxic mother controls how we feel and for how long we feel it. Does it sound familiar?

A child who is repeatedly invalidated, becomes a confused child and a toxic mother constantly invalidates you.

When you're invalidated as a child, and repeatedly told you are worthless, when you're older this is what you believe, and it's very difficult to reverse this feeling recorded in our being.

The invalidated, despised, humiliated, insulted child loses confidence in her feelings. She loses the use of her emotional brain—and the emotional brain is one of the necessary tools for survival.

Examples of invalidation that the toxic mother uses:

- Stop crying, or I'll hit you.

- I've done so much for you.

- You're not worth anything.

- Nobody is going to love you.

- Change your mood!

- Go screaming/crying somewhere else!

- What a bad character you have, nobody will want to be with you.

- You are already making a drama out of it.

- You don't fight enough.

- You are not responsible enough.

- Your room is a disaster.

- You look like a freak (although that day you are wearing your best clothes).

- You are very clumsy.

- I suppose you might be always wrong.

- You never listen.

- Get out.

- Shut up.

- Take it easy.

- It's already happened, it's not that bad.

- Don't bother me.

- You're overreacting.

- You cry for nonsense.

- You could have done better.

- You only give me problems.

- It's your fault

- Your examples. Write in your notebook examples of invalidation that your mother has used with you.

Gas lighting, emotional suffocation

This is one of the most destructive emotional abuse strategies. It's used by our toxic mothers to make us think we're sick in the head.

The toxic mother presents you with false information so that you doubt yourself, and even your sanity. Your mother convinces you that your way of seeing life is not true. So, if you've ever thought you are crazy, no, you're not. It was your mother who made you believe it.

Gaslighting is a form of psychological abuse that consists of presenting false information to make the victim doubt her memory, perception, or her sanity.

The abusive mother may make you wonder:

- Has it really happened?
- What has my mother really done?
- What has my mother said?
- Did I hear her properly?
- Have I not understood something?
- Wasn't I listening when she told me?
- Why do I always get confused?

Doesn't respect your personal boundaries

Personal boundaries are rules or limits that a person creates to identify what are the reasonable, safe and permissible ways for other people to behave around them and how they'll respond when someone steps on those limits. They are rules and principles you live by when you say what you will or won't do or allow.

They're constructed from a mixture of beliefs, opinions, attitudes, past experiences, and social learning.

Personal boundaries define you as an individual, delineating your likes and dislikes, and establishing the distances that you allow others to approach you. They include physical, mental, psychological, and spiritual limits, which include beliefs, emotions, intuitions, and self-esteem.

Personal boundaries are healthy and necessary in a person's life.

As the daughter of a toxic mother, you've been raised to have no limits. Nothing you own is yours, not even your body, certainly not your thoughts and beliefs. You aren't an individual person, separated from your mother; you are an extension of her. Unfortunately, that doesn't change when you're older, and it goes on even if you're 60 years old.

Your mother doesn't respect your physical, emotional, or psychological boundaries. She reads your letters, emails, or asks you exceedingly personal questions. You feel you have no privacy; she rummages in your closets, mail. She sets your time without asking you if it suits you.

One of the problems you have as a daughter of a toxic mother is that you've never been allowed to establish your own boundaries. Your mother has done it for you.

The problem of growing this way is that when you reach adulthood, you don't change: you don't know how to establish and enforce boundaries. So anyone can come and set them up for you: a boss, a couple, even your own children.

Let's see below the different types of boundaries that your mother breaks.

Physical Boundaries

The toxic mother violates your physical space. She thinks she has rights over you, that's why she goes in while you're in the bathroom without asking, or she gets into a private conversation without anyone inviting her. If you move, she'll have the right to enter your home when and however she wants.

Mental Boundaries

Your mother invades your thoughts, opinions, and beliefs. Toxic mothers can't tolerate disagreement. So every time you've tried to express your own thoughts, she has reprimanded you, or worse, she's acted with anger and left you isolated, or ignored.

As a result, you've learned to live without expressing your own reality. Or if you've been the rebel, the scapegoat who has always continued to give her opinions despite knowing that you were going to be reprimanded, then you've always been labeled as the bad one, the cause of all the dysfunction and family problems.

The mental boundaries that your mother has imposed on you are the reason why you need constant approval from those you think are stronger than you. You doubt your thoughts and opinions. You need third parties to validate them.

Emotional Boundaries

The toxic mother limits your ability to have and control your own feelings.

She is only motivated by her wishes, and the people around her are there with the sole purpose of satisfying them.

The narcissistic mother tries to minimize the child's feelings if they are in direct conflict with her own needs. The child will be told that "she really doesn't feel that" or that she will "get over it" or "stop being a baby". She'll say or do anything that makes the child stop being so "dependent" because that requires that she puts her children before her own needs.

This has caused you to have grown up feeling that you're insignificant (your mother has ignored your feelings), and very hurt knowing that your mother has never cared about your true self. Moreover, worst of all, you've believed that your mother's feelings come before your own.

Have you written down all the boundaries your mother has broken with you? Write all the examples that come to your head. Make a list. Remember, she's broken not only the physical limits but also your emotional and mental boundaries. To how many things couldn't you say no?

Do you recognize the consequences of all these lacks of boundaries in your daily behaviors? Having not had intimacy, not having been able to express yourself as you would have liked to because you had to do things her own way, how did it make you feel? Write everything down, so that later you can work on it.

Practices triangulation

Triangulation is a sadistic manipulation method used by a narcissistic person to manipulate two people while creating a triangle with her in the middle.

The triangulation in a dysfunctional family, with a toxic mother, basically consists of the mother competing the brothers and sisters against each other. This feeds envy, anger, and contempt, all highly corrosive emotions, to confront the siblings. Divide and conquer is something this emotional vampire understands.

The toxic mother is responsible for creating jealousy among siblings, through the unfair treatment of one of them (the scapegoat, the hated son/daughter or black sheep of the family) and of arbitrarily rewarding the other, (the golden child, the favorite and loved one). The toxic mother also triangulates through unfair comparisons created with the intention of disuniting the siblings.

Undermines your achievements

The toxic mother won't admit your achievements, except if she can attribute them to herself. Your mother will never let you be the one who appears as the one who does something right. She will attribute your success to her.

If the Sunday roast has gone well, it isn't on your own merits, but because you've used her recipe. If you get good grades, she'll tell everyone because it makes her look like a good mother. If she can't take credit for your achievements, she'll ignore them or despise them.

If you're going to be the center of an event, she won't be there, she'll be late, or she'll act as if it wasn't something so important. Alternatively, she'll make comments like "your brother's graduation was better." Or she'll try to make you feel bad before your big moment starts.

Uses a permissive father

A narcissistic mother can't act alone. She needs a permissive father. One who ends up being submissive to her or loves her to bits.

Within a distorted family with a toxic mother, there is always a permissive father. That father who actively or passively allows the mother to perpetuate her emotional terrorist acts.

So, as the daughter of a toxic mother, you feel like an orphan. Not only have you lacked an affectionate mother, but your father is also like he hadn't been present.

Practices projection

Projection is a dysfunctional tool that the toxic mother uses to put up with her shortcomings and limitations. She projects in you what she is, or what she's jealous of in you. When a toxic mother accuses you of lying, of being unstable, selfish, a bad person…she's accusing you of what she is, she's projecting herself onto you.

To understand it better we'll see what the projection is:

It is a defense mechanism by which the person attributes to other people their defects, thoughts, and even their shortcomings. It's a blame-shifting.

Your mother denies her own qualities and attributes them to you.

Projection can be divided into:

Neurotic projection is about perceiving others in ways that we unconsciously consider criticizable in ourselves. It is when people attribute feelings, attitudes, or motives, they find unacceptable in themselves, to someone else.

It ignores her problem and attributes it to you. It gets rid of that internal load and leaves it outside.

Deflection

Deflection is the art of psychologically and emotionally distracting a person from changing the subject, and focusing the conversation elsewhere. Your mother is the queen of deflection, she practices it so well, that when you're having a conversation with her, you probably end up scratching your head because you don't know what she's talking about.

It's a conversational control method. Clear, simple, and very effective.

Mothers with narcissistic personality disorder are artists of deflection. It's one of their favorite tactics to confuse your mind and make you doubt.

Intimidation. She generates fear.

Intimidation is an act that tries to generate fear in another person so that they do whatever you want. Normally the person who resorts to these tactics doesn't usually use aggression and violence, at least not in an obvious way because their main objective is to manipulate their victim without damaging their image.

It's easy to notice what the abusive person wants because her speech is plagued by indirect threats, which are implicit in her words. She makes it clear to her victim what the consequences of her actions would be and that the responsibility is solely hers. For example, your mum can say: "it's up to you, but I've already told you that you won't do it well", "if you don't do this, I won't buy you new pants."

Blaming to make you feel guilty

Blaming a person is a form of psychological abuse. Some psychologists define it as emotional manipulation.

People who blame know how to make you feel bad. They use guilt to manipulate you to do what they want.

Guilt can be transmitted with words, tone of voice, or even a look. The blamer likes to play dirty. To get away with what she wants, your mother takes advantage of your desire to please her and be a good person.

If your mother is trying to make you feel guilty, part of her behavior may be motivated by her own feelings of guilt that she's not recognized or resolved.

Munchhausen. Syndrome by Proxy.

This actually isn't an abuse technique, but a disorder that your toxic mother can have. However, I've included it in this section because it's a disorder that consists of making children sick, which is a form of abuse.

Munchausen Syndrome by proxy is a disorder in which a person, usually the caregiver or mother of the child, deliberately causes injury, illness, or disorder to another person, usually the child. It's a psychiatric disorder registered in the DSM-V as Factitious, or artificial, disorder.

It's a form of child abuse in which one of the parents causes in the child real or apparent symptoms of a disease.

There are cases in which mothers with a narcissistic personality disorder make their children sick to keep them under their power and thus obtain their narcissistic supply. Sicking their children gratifies their psychological needs for care and dependence.

The Silence Treatment

It is a set of behaviors that aim to ignore the other person. It's a form of covert psychological abuse. An attempt to control and vex others. It constitutes a harmful and toxic behavior that can cause diverse and serious effects in the other person.

Rejection

The toxic mother usually shows a rejection behavior towards the "bad daughter" or scapegoat. She lets you know in a variety of ways, you aren't wanted.

Leaving aside a child's value or belittling their needs is one of the ways of how emotional rejection can happen. Other examples of rejection may include telling a child to leave, insulting him or telling him that he's worthless. The mother will always blame the family problems on the child that becomes the scapegoat of the family.

Other examples of rejection from a mother to her children are:

- Constant criticism.
- Abuse.
- Telling the child that he/she is ugly, or messing with his/her physical appearance.
- Shout or curse directed at the child.
- Frequent disparagement and use of labels like "stupid" or "idiot."
- Constant degrading jokes.
- Verbal humiliation
- Constant teasing about the body type of the child.
- Rejecting hugs and affectionate gestures.
- Excluding the child from family activities.
- Expressing regret about the child's sex or even that he/she was not born.
- Expelling the child from the family.

- Your own examples. What forms of rejection have you experienced? In which ways has your mother made you feel like you were not part of the family? Write on your notebook everything that comes to your mind.

Exploitation and physical violence

Exploitation can be considered manipulation, as it is the act of using a minor for personal advantage. A narcissistic mother takes advantage of her children in different ways.

Giving a child responsibilities that are much greater than those of a child's age is exploitation. Using a child for profit is abusive and is also another act of exploitation.

Although most mothers with narcissistic personality disorder are quite well disguised, and their "tortures" aren't visible for people outside the family, there are some that use more easily detectable methods.

Some of the habitual acts of exploitation for a narcissistic mother are:

A child who becomes a "caretaker" of his mother.

Making the child feel she is expected to take care of the other younger siblings.

Blaming a child for the bad behavior of the other siblings.

Giving unreasonable responsibilities to a child.

Encouraging participation in pornography.

Allowing her children to be sexually abused by partners or family members.

Perspecticide, brainwashing

One of the most dangerous manipulation techniques is to change the victim's way of perceiving herself.

The word "perspecticide" has been used to refer to the brainwashing to which prisoners of war were subjected, and its use is spreading in psychology to refer to the brainwashing of a person abusing his/her victim.

The objective of the perspecticide is to achieve a total loss of identity in the victim. The toxic mother doesn't want you to think for yourself; she'll try to erase your identity.

Perspecticide always implies an abusive relationship, control and manipulation, so that over time, the narcissistic person changes her victim's way of thinking.

Your narcissistic mother ends up defining your world. She defines what love is for you, how you handle your relationships and even how you should think or dress.

Some examples are:

Deciding how the victims should invest their time.

Obsessive control over everyday detail.

Change of self-concept. The narcissistic person makes sure to "steal" the victim's self-concept, placing her own in its place. This way, the perception of the victim changes, who begins to see herself with the eyes of the other person.

The person with narcissistic personality disorder decides on her victim, how she has to dress, what kind of work she takes, and how she has to behave.

Cognitive empathy

I know that you've always heard that narcissists don't have empathy. However, empathy can be good or bad.

According to the dictionary, empathy is defined as: 'the ability to understand and share the feelings of another.'

The definition doesn't mention anything about experiencing compassion, remorse, or humanity.

There are different types of empathy:

- Emotional empathy occurs when you feel the same pain of those around you even if you are not experiencing pain. (You cry when your friend's dog has died)

- Compassionate empathy: you understand a person's difficulties, but, as you aren't experiencing them, you can act and help to improve the situation.

- Cognitive empathy: you perceive and understand the emotions of another. Cognitive empathy implies having a piece of more complete and accurate knowledge about the contents of another person's mind, including how the person feels. Cognitive empathy is more of a skill and you can train and develop it. It's a well-developed ability in skilled marketers and many lawyers who use it to get what they want. Moreover, of course, it's a skill that the narcissist excels at.

Compartmentalization

According to Wikipedia compartmentalization is "An unconscious psychological defense mechanism used to avoid cognitive dissonance or mental discomfort and anxiety caused by a person who has values, cognitions, emotions, beliefs, etc. in conflict with each other. Compartmentalization allows these conflicting ideas to coexist, inhibiting direct or explicit recognition and interaction between separate compartmentalized ego states."

In summary and applied to the narcissistic mother, she changes her entire focus to a situation in question and suppresses the feelings that usually accompany it (a popular example of compartmentalization is that of soldiers on the battlefield who put aside any guilt associated with killing people when they are in combat.)

Hoovering, she tries to suck you back

When your mother feels your distance from her, and she loses control over you, she tries to suck you back into the cage. She doesn't do it because she is repentant, or because she loves you, but because she needs to control you to inflate her ego.

Your mother will use your emotional weaknesses to bring you back. (She blackmails you emotionally by making you feel bad so you come back). As you will see later when you begin to see the aftermath that the abuse has left you, you try to get apart from her, but at that moment she gives you something good to attract you back. Manipulating you emotionally, she creates a traumatic bond with you that keeps you close to her.

Victimization

When all the manipulation tactics we've seen fail, your mother resorts to victimhood. She passes all the responsibility to you and resorts to emotional blackmail, pretending to be the victim of the situation. She victimizes to the point that you end up feeling bad for your behavior, when in fact you haven't done anything wrong.

Being "the victim" your mother, the abuser, generates a feeling of guilt in you that keeps you trapped in her net.

The empathy that characterizes you makes you fall into her trap and, by becoming the "bad guy" of the movie, you're more inclined to give in to her demands—this way she manipulates you without you being aware of it.

Revenge or harassment

If your toxic mother can't change you or make you return with her, then she'll change how others see you. Revenge. It looks like it, and it is.

The abuser can't bear to be abandoned, and that's when she loses her mind and tries to torment you.

She'll try to attack you socially, morally, and physically. Any way to hurt you is valid. Her ego is so hurt that she only seeks revenge.

When you separate from your mother because you see everything she's done to you, you expect her to react and somehow show some tenderness, some maternal instinct. Nothing could be further away from the truth. Like any other person with a narcissistic personality disorder, when you leave her, she'll try to hurt you as much as she can.

Chapter 8: Protection Tips

> **narcissist filter:** what they accuse others of is actually an unconscious admission of their own character

Many people think that schizophrenia, stress, anxiety, and depression are the only kinds of mental health problems, but the list is a lot longer. Eating disorders, borderline personality disorder, bipolar disorder are all mental health problems.

Personality disorders are just a subcategory of mental health problems. People who have these disorders have unhealthy thinking and thought patterns. They will have behavioral problems, too. These thinking patterns are very rigid, and it takes much therapy to change and challenge these patterns with time. Many people who have this disorder will have problems perceiving and relating to situations and people.

Causes of NPD

Nobody really knows what causes NPD. It isn't easy to ask what causes mental health problems like depression. Some people are more susceptible than others. With NPD, some have it while others don't. Some will have a little; others will have an extreme case. It is a mystery, but studies suggest that the following problems might be some risk factors that can cause NPD later in life:

- Unrealistic expectations.
- Hereditary problems like oversensitivity and genes.
- Trauma early in life.
- Negative experiences in childhood like poor parenting or abuse.
- Experienced a lot of criticism.
- Psychological problems.

Narcissists are made. They aren't born that way. While genes do play a part, it is thought that experiences have more influence on developing NPD. It won't happen overnight but can happen at any age. It mostly happens during childhood because of poor parenting like over praising, over-pampering, being insensitive or from negative experiences.

Diagnostic Criteria

Diagnosis of narcissism is hard, and since most people who have this problem don't look for help, most doctors don't have a lot of experience in diagnosing the condition. Most doctors will refer the person to a mental health professional. In order for them to be diagnosed properly with NPD, they will have to meet five or more of the following:

- Being arrogant regularly.

- Having an exaggerated sense of self-importance.

- Believing others are jealous of them.

- Needing excessive admiration and compliments.

- Being jealous of others.

- Extreme sense of entitlement.

- Lack of empathy.

- Exploits and takes advantage of others.

Thoughts and Actions of Narcissists

Trying to get into a narcissist's mind is hard to do. Everyone acts and thinks differently, and each person is unique in the way they react and approach situations. A narcissist has a set behavioral pattern, and this makes them stand out. While there might be some anomalies in place since everybody is different, there are two examples:

- Using Covert or Overt Methods

For a narcissist to manipulate a situation or person so their needs are met, they might use methods that are described as either overt or covert. Overt is very obvious, where covert methods are very secretive and slide under the radar. Covert methods are very destructive to others, and this is why people who are in a relationship with a narcissist have problems leaving. They begin to questions whether it is them or me. A classic method is gaslighting.

A normal narcissist will always use overt methods. A vulnerable narcissist is going to use covert methods. A malignant or toxic narcissist is going to use a mixture of both.

- Cerebral or Somatic Approach

This is talking about the way a narcissist appreciates themselves and things. A narcissist who uses somatic methods will be totally taken with how they look, their general appearance, and their body. They are extremely vain. The cerebral method is using their brain, and seeming to be very intelligent. This narcissist will take great lengths to convince others that their opinion is needed and the only one that matters.

It is important to identify the type of narcissist that you are dealing with. While it could be hard to pinpoint exactly, you should be able to identify the dangerous type. A malignant or toxic narcissist won't have any problem hurting other people and won't show any remorse. This narcissist damages everybody around them. Anybody who is lucky enough to get out of a relationship with this type of narcissist is going to need a lot of emotional support or therapy after.

You may be reading this and wondering how anybody can't see there are things wrong with how they are thinking and acting. This is exactly how NPD works. You have to remember that narcissism is a personality disorder, and this creates a warped way of thinking. Narcissists will completely 100 percent think that you are wrong, and you should see their uniqueness. You shouldn't argue with them since they are always right. They will never look at themselves and think that they might be wrong. They might think that they would have handled the situation differently and better. True narcissists don't see a problem with how they act or think. When dealing with a malignant or toxic narcissist, these people don't see a problem with hurting others for their own gain.

Why A Narcissist Won't Get Treated

Many narcissists won't realize that there is a problem. If somebody tells them they should seek help since they are showing narcissistic behaviors, they will laugh or turn it around on you.

This isn't true for everybody. If a person has a mild form of narcissism, there could be an "aha" moment where they might think: "hey, I wonder if this applies to me?" when they are reading about narcissism or if somebody points out they are showing narcissistic behaviors. This is extremely rare and it is unlikely that a vulnerable or classic narcissist will ever seek help.

Will they get help? With some, they will but only after they have self-destructed or hurt someone close to them very badly. If a moment pushes them to a point, it might be that medical help might be accepted. In spite of all that, it is still unlikely, and it is a very sad fact.

Will Treatment Help?

There are various treatments for narcissism, but many centers around challenging thought patterns and behavioral changes. In extreme cases, it might be recommended that they are hospitalized, especially for extreme narcissists who have become very self-destructive.

The biggest problem is that treatment centers focus around solving the incident instead of solving the condition.

Can treatment help? It could, if they seek help, but it will take a lot of commitment and effort on the narcissist's part. Treatment isn't easy, and this goes for any type of problem that requires challenging thoughts and mindsets along with cognitive behavioral therapy. This treatment method won't be successful overnight and is going to require a long time along with maintenance treatment after that.

Personality Disorders Like Narcissism

Many mental health problems and personality disorders are linked together in some way. A person that suffers from depression could also have anxiety. A person who has stress could also suffer from anxiety. A person who has been diagnosed with bipolar disorder might have narcissistic behaviors. A person who has been diagnosed with a borderline personality disorder might have NPD, too.

In spite of all of that, there are three personality disorder that link closely to NPD:

- Histrionic personality disorder

- Antisocial personality disorder

- Borderline personality disorder

A healthcare professional can assess if a certain type of disorder is there, but talking someone into seeking help is hard, especially if they have narcissism.

Dealing with the Abuser

Now that you have decided to cut ties with your narcissist, you might be wondering if it is fine to remain friends with this person? In specific cases, it could be impossible to totally shut the door on your abuser even if you want to. Immediate family, friends, and coworkers that you have to see constantly will have a presence in your life.

Can you still be nice to them? The answer is no and yes. First, nobody expects you to "clean things up" with your abuser. If you feel that remaining civil would work best, them it could work out. While we are on the topic of being civil, is it possible to be civil to a narcissist. It is questionable if they can understand or adapt to that.

Resuming a relationship after a fight with a narcissist will take repentance and an apology from the offender, and, remember that a narcissist won't ever take the blame for anything, even if you know they did it. Without apologizing, the narcissist won't even think about being civil.

What does this mean for you? Simply that trying to have a "civil" relationship may be one-sided. Unfortunately, your abuser might take this opportunity to embarrass you if you try to initiate contact.

You could try to reach out and talk about the upcoming family reunion, but they might totally ignore or dismiss you once you begin talking. This is something they might do if there are other people around that see they are treating you with hatred.

Seeing as the narcissist has a pristine image with the other people who are around you, the people that see you being treated negatively will take the narcissist's side, that is if you did something wrong.

In many cases, the best thing to do after ending a relationship of any kind with a narcissist is to avoid them completely. Ignoring and treating them like a non-entity could be more beneficial for your emotional and mental healing. This will keep you from being drawn back into their trap. It also makes sure your abuse won't be able to exploit you.

Is it going to be easy? No. Most narcissistic abuse victims say the urge to reach out and talk or to ask forgiveness could pop up at any moment while you are healing from the abuse. This might even happen years after you have left the relationship.

Even though it may be hard, it isn't impossible. Try the following strategies to help you heal and strengthen your resolve to keep your distance from the abuser:

- Get Rid of All Communication

Block. Unfriend. Unfollow. This may sound harsh, but in this digital age, it is the worst thing you could do to somebody who is on social media. You also have to cut all ties that you have, or they could try to reach you in other ways to try and rekindle the relationship.

What if I really have to speak with them? Don't allow this thought to drive you to open ways of communication. What is important right now is you. You have to keep your focus on recovering. Make sure not to leave any windows or doors open and don't allow any opportunities to let your internal mechanism push you into a conversation.

- Don't Update Your Life on Social Media

Nowadays, it's easy to find information on anybody's current activities and preoccupations. They don't call it the internet superhighway for no reason. The bad news is this could make it easier to keep checking on your abuser by getting tidbits of information on their life.

The biggest problem with stalking them online is it could spark flames. One flame is longing: the more you look at their updates and photos, the more you want to be back in their lives. The other flame is sadness: you see their life is going on without you, and the fact they aren't seemingly affected by your absence could injure your self-worth.

You need to remember that narcissists are masters of disguise. They are great at pretending. Your absence might have caused them some distress; they will make sure not to show you this. They are expecting you to look at their life. They have made sure to have images ready to hit you with.

- Think about the Truth

Even if you know you are right, you have a tendency to give other people the benefit of the doubt. This is just how reasonable people are. Even if you are dealing with an abuser, victims need to look at other angles. They might be hurting as well. They might have low self-esteem. They might be troubled.

Nobody other than you deserves your kindness and compassion. Narcissists aren't troubled people. They don't want to be fixed. They aren't acting out of trauma. This is the problem with narcissism. They don't "deserve" the compassion that most of us give to others.

Narcissists think they are better than others because they were brought up to believe they are. They fight to control everybody in their lives since they feel like they are entitled to power. They often think: "I am better than you, therefore you should listen to me so you can somehow achieve the same greatness." It is a completely toxic mentality.

Don't try to make sense of why they are acting the way they do. Try to think about the truth behind the actions. Yes, it is going to hurt at the beginning to see the behavior for what it really is, but make your mind see the truth, and it will be easier to keep your distance when they lose their luster and take on their true form in your mind.

- Stay Preoccupied

There isn't any strategy that is more effective that just keeping your abuser out of your mind. Your focus needs to be on you so do things that show yourself that you love yourself. When you constantly think about the painful abuse, it can be very negative if done to excess.

Take yourself out on a date, find a new hobby, and buy yourself something new. It will be better if you can find something you enjoy without needing anyone else's company. The more you can show yourself love, the faster you will find your self-worth. When that is in place, it will be easier to see the abuser for what they really are. This lets you detach yourself from your abuser further.

Chapter 9: Separating From a Narcissistic Mother

> Your life will get better when you realize it's better to be alone than chase around people who don't give two fucks about you

Trying to handle an extreme and unhealthy narcissist mother isn't easy, whether you decide to stay in their lives or walk away.

If you make the decision to walk away and cut ties, the way you handle this move is important to consider. If your narcissist mother isn't abusive, being considerate and empathetic will make sure you can leave feeling good about your decision. Just keep in mind that narcissist mothers can't empathize at times, and this is because of heightened sensitivity. If you can let them down easy without exposing or confronting them, this might be the best thing to keep their self-esteem from suffering a massive blow. If abuse is present in the relationship, you have to cut the relationship quickly or in a safe way that is expedient for you.

If your Narcissist Mother Returns

Just like any person who has been involved in a relationship, your narcissist mother will probably try to contact you. They could be suspicious, angry, or hurt about why you aren't in their lives anymore depending on them and the relationship. This is understandable.

If you decided to quit talking to your parent since their actions were damaging to your well-being, their parental love isn't going to just disappear. Some people claim that narcissists don't love, but this really isn't the case. They just can't show or express their love in front of other people. Some narcissists mothers find they have loving feelings emerge when they aren't around their narcissistic supply.

They could contact you in a human manner that is caring, to gloat, or in an attempt to get you back or get something from you. Every situation, just like every individu,al, will be different. If at all possible, to respond to these attempted contacts, please remember to have empathy, but deliver it in a way that doesn't invite doubt, questions, or hope. Stand by what you know is best and be firm instead of being open to the things they might offer you.

If you left a relationship you had with an emotionally abusive narcissist, you might find they will get in touch with you in the future. It is advisable that you refuse contact instead of trying to reason or discuss things with them. No good will ever come from these interactions, just more harm. If they continue to contact you, and get angry, abusive, or emotional, not reacting might force them to get control of themselves and move on.

If you have taken some distance from a family member who isn't abusive but has unhealthy narcissistic tendencies, you might take an opportunity to have a conversation. This doesn't mean you will be opening yourself up for danger but means you are trying to be present in their lives as long as they can behave themselves. If they still can't behave, you might have to figure out if you want to increase distance or continue the relationship.

No Contact

Having no contact doesn't mean it is temporary. It means leaving for good and not looking back, ever. Many people don't like the term no contact since it can easily be misconstrued as just temporarily not having communication. The bad news is narcissists are like tumors that are cancerous. They have to be removed entirely and swiftly from our lives. If this tumor isn't removed quickly, it could spread or grow into different organs. There are times when we have to cut all ties forever. This no contact phase is like rehab for the victims of narcissistic abuse. You have to have complete isolation to cleanse yourself of the narcissistic energy.

Saying goodbye is having the ability to completely let go of this toxic individual without having second thoughts or guilt. You don't have to follow them on social media, be their friend, or check in on them. Severing all ties is the only way you can move forward after being in a relationship with a narcissist mother. Having a relationship with narcissists mothers is an addiction that has been confused with love. When you are in rehab, you have to make sure you have complete isolation from all drugs to get back control of your live. It is essential to have a support system with family and friends.

If you have had a relationship with a narcissist mother and burned bridges with friends and family, finding an online or offline abuse recovery support group will work wonders. If your insurance covers behavioral health, you need to make an appointment with a psychologist as quickly as you can after the relationship has ended. Therapy will help you with self-esteem and find the reasons why you let them abuse you. Addressing these issues is the only way to resolve them completely. Look at it as an investment in you psychological portfolio.

Chapter 10: How to HEAL from ABUSE!

> You were not weak
> You just loved
> Without boundaries

Healing from Experience with a Narcissist

You know what narcissism is and you know how to deal with it. The next step is making sure that you have what is needed to truly heal from the experience. This is a process, and no one expects you to just forget the issue never happened. Working on yourself and putting yourself first is what will allow you to get over the negative consequences of your experience

Personal Self-Esteem

When someone has low self-esteem, they are more vulnerable to narcissists and other people and situations that are largely negative. In fact, narcissists look for those with low self-esteem because they know that it will make it easier to get them into their web. When you have good self-esteem, you have a healthy level of self-respect and confidence in your abilities and worth. When self-esteem is low, someone is more likely to tolerate abusive situations, not live up to their potential and become depressed.

When you have high self-esteem, you:

- Feel accepted and valued by others.

- Respect and accept yourself even when you are making mistakes.

- Recognize your positive qualities.

- Think positively concerning yourself.

- Feel worthy of being given respect and fairness by others.

- Believe in yourself and do not allow setbacks or failure stop you from pursuing your goals.

- Take pride in what you do.

Low self-esteem is characterized by:

- Putting more focus on your failures instead of your accomplishments.

- Feeling inferior or insecure.

- Feeling that others will automatically not accept you.

- Thinking negatively about yourself.

- Being very hard on yourself when it is not warranted.

- Feeling like you do not deserve good things because you think you are defective in some way.

- Doubting your ability to be successful.

Self-esteem is a part of everything that you do in life. It affects your performance at school, work and in your relationships. Low self-esteem can also stop you from living a full life since it is characterized by fear of trying new things or testing your limits.

Where Self-Esteem Comes From

Self-esteem ultimately comes from within. However, there are a number of factors that can influence it. The people around you play a role in how you see yourself. This is especially true when it comes to those close to you and those you respect. For example, if a parent is constantly critical of a child, this can damage the child's self-esteem. On the other hand, when a parent is very supportive, it helps someone to see their own value which leads to healthy self-esteem.

Every person has that inner voice that essentially tells them what to think of themselves. For some, this inner voice can be highly negative and critical. When this happens, it is easy to believe the voice and feel as though you are inferior. It is common to have negative feelings, but when you allow them to dominate, you eventually start believing them. It is important to listen to negative inner feelings, but then put them into perspective. For example, you did poorly on a test, so naturally, this is upsetting. If your inner voice tells you that you are a failure and you listen to it and do not question it, you will start to believe this, resulting in lower self-esteem.

Comparing yourself to other people is another influencer on your self-esteem. It is fine to evaluate those around you, but do not allow this to overshadow your strengths. Taking inventory of your weaknesses and strengths and focusing on what you are good at can help prevent the strengths of those around you from negatively impacting how you view yourself.

Other factors that can alter your self-esteem include:

- How people react to you.

- Illness, injury, and disability.

- Status and role in society.

- Your personal life experiences.

- Age.

- Media messages.

The media is a major influencer. For example, you see all of these seemingly perfect people in magazines and on television. It is natural for people to compare themselves and believe that what they are seeing is what they need to be. This can be especially damaging to younger children and those who already have low self-esteem. It is important to remember that every person is unique and there is no right way to look.

Improving Your Self-Esteem

The good news is that if you have low self-esteem, this does not have to remain so. There are ways to boost it and alleviate the negative thoughts and feelings from dominating your view of yourself. To get started, work on developing life skills that contribute to how you see yourself and the world around you. These include:

• Do not be afraid to identify and experience your feelings. When you push feelings down and try to ignore them, they will eventually come to the surface.

• Do not be afraid to detach yourself from negative situations and people.

• Be receptive to those around you and empathize with people.

• Think optionally and not in black and white. This allows you to solve problems better and learn new things.

• Be assertive when it is needed. Do not allow others to dictate the direction of your life.

Focus on the good things in your life and what you are good at. Low self-esteem can make it seem like you are not good enough at anything. However, when you reflect on the good, it makes it easier to remember that it does exist on days when you are feeling down.

Make a learning opportunity out of every mistake. Every person fails and makes mistakes. This is part of life. However, do not dwell on these and the negative consequences that might come with them. Spend an hour being upset because it is important to experience your emotions. However, after an hour, go into action mode and consider why the mistake or failure occurred. You will always be able to find at least one lesson. This lesson reduces the risk of mistakes and failure in the future.

Know that perfection is simply not possible. What is important is that you are putting in the effort and working to learn and get better. No person is born automatically being great at everything. Life is all about learning and working on developing the skills needed to achieve your goals.

Remember that every person has their own strengths. Imagine a world where every person is just good at everything. There would be no healthy competition, no learning, and no balance. Know your strengths and respect the strengths of others.

Know what you cannot change. For example, if you are short, you are short. You cannot change this. Once you accept what cannot be changed, you can start putting your focus on the areas of your life that can be improved.

Do not be afraid to try. You never know what you are good at until you test your limits. Have you always wanted to play soccer, but were afraid you were not good enough? Get a game going with friends or join a local team. You may be great, or you may not. Either way, you tried it, and every new thing you try expands your horizons.

Give yourself credit when you deserve it. When you do something great, be proud of yourself. It is easy to put more focus on flaws because this is just what humans do. However, when you switch your focus to the good stuff, your self-esteem will get a boost.

How to Heal from Narcissism in Your Life

Dealing with a narcissist in your life can be damaging, and it allows for a flood of negativity in your life. Once the narcissist is gone, the issues you faced do not just disappear with them. You have to take the time to heal, and this can take some time. Give yourself time and be patient with yourself. There are stages that you go through during the healing process. Learning more about these allow you to ensure that you are doing everything needed to truly heal.

During the first stage, denial is common. You do not want to believe that the narcissist in your life is a toxic person. You may make excuses for their behavior and not want to admit that they are not healthy for you. Start writing down your thoughts concerning their treatment of you. Every few days, look back at what you wrote. This allows you to identify the pattern.

The second stage involves getting to know more about narcissism. This allows you to see what they do, and it allows you to realize that they are not capable of empathy and healthy relationships. This is a hard lesson to learn, but it is imperative for you to heal.

The third stage starts the separation process. Write a letter telling the narcissist in your life that you are walking away. Be detailed about why you are walking away. Now, you will not send the letter. This is for you to find some closure as you end the relationship.

For stage four, you cut the person from your life. Once you say "goodbye" you have to remain strong. Cut off all contact and do not give into them no matter what. It is common for a narcissist to try and manipulate you back into their life. You should consider a clean break. This means that you just cut off contact and never go back. Since this requires taking your attention away from them, expect them to try and contact you. They can be very persistent. Just make sure that you never respond.

Stage five involves taking a deep look at why you started a relationship with them in the first place. What was it about the narcissist that made you want them in your life? This can help you to prevent a future experience with a narcissist. It also lets you reflect and determine if your reasons for a relationship with them are things you need to work on. For example, was your self-esteem low when you started spending time with them? If so, improving your self-esteem can prevent a future narcissist experience.

The sixth stage is all about you. You want to evaluate your weaknesses and your self-worth. Find places that need improvement and dedicate yourself to working on them. After having a narcissist in your life, it is common to be in a negative place. Take small steps to essentially recover from your experience. Every person gets through their steps in their own time. Do not rush and do not get discouraged if you are going through the motions slowly. Every day is another day without narcissism in your life.

The seventh and final stage is accepting that the situation happened and committing yourself to learning from it. Use the pain and negativity that the narcissist caused in your life to be stronger and to drive you to put the focus on self-care. You do not need anyone in your life that contributes anything negative. Remember this. You are valuable and worthy. You also want to truly forgive yourself.

How to Handle Future Narcissism in Your Life

This ultimately comes down to knowing your worth and putting up your boundaries with any narcissist you might meet in the future. With improved self-esteem and knowing how to approach those who are narcissistic, you can better avoid falling into their web and having your life filled with their negativity.

First and foremost, make a pact with yourself that you will never allow another narcissist to take control of you. You are valuable, and your worth is determined by you and not them. They can quickly worm their way into your life because they are charming. It is easy not to believe a narcissist is a narcissist at first. They can be initially nice, or at least seem that way based on their actions and their desire to control and manipulate you.

Consider your past experience with a narcissist. Do you remember how the relationship began? Look for similar patterns with any new person in your life whom you think might be a narcissist. Remembering history is one of the best ways to prevent issues from your past from repeating themselves. It can be hard to spot the signs at first, so be diligent and do not discount your feelings if you think another narcissist has entered your life.

Go to your support system and people you trust. Ask their opinion about the person you think might be a narcissist. In many cases, when you are getting close to someone, it can be difficult to see their flaws. However, your close friends and family are on the outside looking it and can pick up on issues faster and easier than you can. Just remember that if their opinions are negative, do not get defensive. They care about you and want to ensure that you are surrounded by good people.

Practice regular self-care. When you are taking care of yourself and putting yourself first, you are less vulnerable to the charms and manipulations of a narcissist. There are numerous ways to practice self-care. You can choose one or several methods depending on your needs and what you want. The following are common self-care methods to consider:

• Make your schedule simpler so that you can put more focus on the activities that make you happy and alleviate your stress.

• Take a warm bath, and use this time to read a book, listen to your favorite songs, or just kick back. Make sure the atmosphere is relaxing and that this is time just for you. Turn off your phone and eliminate any distractions.

• Get some physical activity since this will help to boost your physical, mental, and emotional health. It is a good way to blow off some steam. Any type of physical activity that you enjoy will provide you with benefits.

- Create a list of what you are grateful for. A narcissist can take away your joy, so sometimes you need to remind yourself of the things in your life that are great.

- Find a mentor that can aid you in getting to know yourself and guide you through difficult times. This can be a religious leader, a therapist, or any person in this realm.

- Take a day to unplug from everything. Turn off all electronics and go back to a simpler time. Take a walk or a nap, enjoy favorite foods, play games with friends, or anything else that does not require electronics.

- Try something new. Have you been wanting to start painting or write a book? Is there a type of cuisine you have not tried before? As long as it is something new to you, do it. This gets you out of your comfort zone and expands your horizons.

- Go dancing. Just like physical activity, dancing can alleviate stress, and it contributes to greater well-being. Hit a club with friends or crank up some tunes in your living room and dance it out.

- Get out in nature. Nature indeed has a way to make you feel calmer and more relaxed. It is also quiet and allows you to engage in self-reflection. A quick walk or hike is a great place to start.

- Learn how to meditate. Even just five minutes of meditation per day can help to keep you grounded and it makes it easier to deal with stressors.

- Start a journal to keep track of your thoughts and feelings.

- Eliminate the clutter in your living space. When your home is more organized and clean, this helps to make you calmer. Clutter naturally induces feelings of stress.

- Make sure to get adequate sleep. Get yourself on a regular sleeping schedule and stick to it. If you want to take a nap during the day, keep it to an hour or less so that it does not interfere with your ability to sleep at night.

Conclusion

> *The truth will always come out. Don't miss it when it does.*

Narcissism is affecting more and more people in the world today. If narcissism was a rare occurance in the past, incidences are on a steady and dangerous rise right now. What makes this rise faster than it should is social media.

It has increased your chances of meeting with a narcissist significantly. Be ready to handle any challenge they might throw at you. If you must live with a narcissist, it is imperative that you take appropriate steps to secure your safety. Be prepared for all of his outbursts of rage.

Narcissists can be extremely charming and are master manipulators. So be ready and vigilant for any scam they might try to pull over you. It is easy to lapse into a narcissistic personality nowadays. Taking a few selfies or making a few self-appraising comments on social media need not necessarily turn you into a modern-day Narcissus. However, it would be best for your interests if you kept such interactions to a bare minimum.

No one is going to assess your worth by going through your Facebook or Twitter profile. Keep your emotions intact. Do not drift off into a stage where you don't care about anyone but yourself. Indulging in luxuries may be a necessary addition to certain lifestyles. Make sure that you always value people and relationships above all things material.

Made in United States
Troutdale, OR
01/25/2024